# Take &Read

# The Gospel of Mark

*Adrian Graffy*

Published in 2009 by Alive Publishing Ltd.
Graphic House, 124 City Road, Stoke on Trent, ST4 2PH.
Tel: +44 (0) 1782 745600   Fax: +44 (0) 1782 745500
www.alivepublishing.co.uk

©2009 Alive Publishing
British Library Catalogue-in-Publication Data.
A catalogue record for this book is available from the British Library.

First published in 2005 by Matthew James Publishing Ltd, Chelmsford.
In the United Kingdom such licences are issued by
The Publishers Licencing Society Ltd, 90 Tottenham Court Road, London W1P 9HE.

First published in 2005 © Department for Catholic Education and Formation, Bishops' Conference of England and Wales.

ISBN 978-1-906278-04-5

Cover image & previous page: Cott Nero DIV f.93v St. Mark's portrait page 45:St Mark, c.698 AD (manuscript) by Eadfrith, Bishop of Lindisfarne.

# Contents

# Foreword

One of the features of the Church of today is the rediscovery of the Bible. In the years since the Second Vatican Council this thirst for the Scriptures has become stronger and stronger. The desire for a deeper engagement with the Bible is clear from the enormous popularity of publications such as *Walk with Me* and *Bible Alive*.

*Take and Read* is designed to assist people in their need to understand the Bible more deeply. The series has been developed as a follow-up to the document 'The Gift of Scripture', which was produced in 2005 by the Bishops of England and Wales, and of Scotland, to mark the 40th anniversary of the Council document on Divine Revelation, *Dei Verbum*.

The story of the conversion of Saint Augustine to the Catholic faith inspired the title of the series. He recounts in his 'Confessions' how he heard a voice calling to him with the words *Tolle, lege* 'Take and Read'. At that moment he picked up the New Testament and read the first chapter his eyes fell upon, from the Letter to the Romans. His conversion was assured.

These books are a major new resource for prayerful reading of the Scriptures both for groups and for individuals. Passages from the Gospels are accompanied by commentary, quotations from the Fathers and from Church documents, Christian art and inspiring photographs, as well as suggestions for prayer and reflection.

It is a great pleasure to acknowledge the work of those who helped develop this series. Representatives from dioceses throughout Britain worked on the preparatory stages. Particular thanks should go to Anne White, Anne Dixon and Sister Vicky Hummell. I record my gratitude to the authors who have produced such rich commentary on the gospel passages. I am particularly pleased that Mike and Sue Conway of Alive Publishing agreed to publish the *Take and Read* series.

*Take and Read* will help you to delve more deeply into the Scriptures, to understand them better, and to pray with the Scriptures. *Take and Read* will assist you in *lectio divina*, that prayerful reading of Scripture which has always been central to the life of the Church.

*Fr Adrian Graffy*

And behold I heard a voice from a nearby house singing and frequently repeating, like a boy or a girl, I do not know which: Take and read; take and read. I grabbed the book and opened it and I read in silence the first chapter my eyes fell upon.

*Augustine Confessions VIII, 29*

I pray you, good Jesus,
that as you have graciously granted me to take
in with delight
the words that give knowledge of you,
so you will grant me in your kindness
to come at last to you, the source of all wisdom,
and to stand for ever before your face. Amen.

*The Prayer of St Bede (to end a session)*

# Introduction

The Gospel of Mark, the shortest of the four gospels, is generally considered to be the first written gospel. The good news of Jesus was at first proclaimed by word of mouth by the followers of Jesus. St Paul says: 'Christ sent me to proclaim the gospel.' (1 Corinthians 1:17) Later on, the gospel was written down to provide accounts of the life, death and resurrection of Jesus. What was proclaimed by word of mouth was written down in order to be passed on to future generations.

So how did Mark compile his gospel? He brought together material which had been preached and turned it into a continuous narrative of the life of Jesus. It is traditionally believed that Mark was an assistant of St Peter in Rome, and it seems quite plausible that Mark records what Peter preached about Jesus. There is an emphasis on the willingness of Jesus to accept death on the cross, and on the difficulty the disciples had in accepting the crucifixion of the Messiah. This theme was of considerable relevance to Christians facing persecution and martyrdom.

Mark puts the gospel together in a very deliberate way.  He beings with Jesus' ministry of preaching and healing in the northern region of Galilee. He then shows how Jesus travels south to the city of Jerusalem, where he continues his ministry until his death and resurrection. Mark has constructed the gospel story in such a way that persecuted Christians will feel encouraged in their fidelity to Christ.

In this book you will find twelve sessions, each presenting a section of the gospel for study and prayer. These twelve sections will give you a good idea of Mark's gospel story and help you to understand it more deeply, but it will help you further if you use your own Bible to read the intervening sections of the gospel which are not contained in the book.

The Gospel of Mark presents Jesus to us in a fresh and exciting way. In it Jesus throws down the challenge of discipleship. That same call to generosity of spirit and fidelity amid trials, the challenge to live by the gospel, is always before us.

Facing page: Christ the Redeemer, Source of Life, c.1393-94 (tempera on panel) by Byzantine artist.

# Mark Introduces Jesus

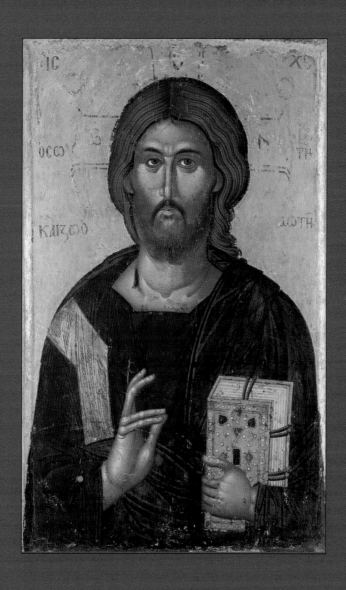

# Hear the Word of God

## Read Mark 1: 1-15

[1] The beginning of the good news of Jesus Christ, the Son of God.

[2] As it is written in the prophet Isaiah, 'See, I am sending my messenger ahead of you, who will prepare your way; [3] the voice of one crying out in the wilderness: 'Prepare the way of the Lord, make his paths straight'.'

[4] John the baptizer appeared in the wilderness, proclaiming a baptism of repentance for the forgiveness of sins. [5] And people from the whole Judean countryside and all the people of Jerusalem were going out to him, and were baptized by him in the river Jordan, confessing their sins.

[6] Now John was clothed with camel's hair, with a leather belt around his waist, and he ate locusts and wild honey.

[7] He proclaimed, 'The one who is more powerful than I is coming after me; I am not worthy to stoop down and untie the thong of his sandals. [8] I have baptized you with water; but he will baptize you with the Holy Spirit.'

[9] In those days Jesus came from Nazareth of Galilee and was baptized by John in the Jordan. [10] And just as he was coming up out of the water, he saw the heavens torn apart and the Spirit descending like a dove on him. [11] And a voice came from heaven, 'You are my Son, the Beloved; with you I am well pleased.'

[12] And the Spirit immediately drove him out into the wilderness. [13] He was in the wilderness forty days, tempted by Satan; and he was with the wild beasts; and the angels waited on him.

[14] Now after John was arrested, Jesus came to Galilee, proclaiming the good news of God, [15] and saying, 'The time is fulfilled, and the kingdom of God has come near; repent, and believe in the good news.'

# Understand the Word of God

**This session will explore:**

- ❖ Mark's presentation of Jesus
- ❖ how Mark proclaims Jesus as the fulfilment of Jewish hopes
- ❖ titles given to Jesus and opening stories about him
- ❖ the Kingdom of God in the preaching of Jesus
- ❖ the message for today.

## Setting in the Gospel

The verses we are reading and studying are the opening verses of the Gospel according to Mark. Right at the start Mark puts the spotlight on the central figure, Jesus, whom he calls 'Christ' and 'Son of God'. What is proclaimed in the first verse will be the theme of the entire Gospel of Mark. The verses which speak of the Baptism of Jesus, the Temptation, and his preaching of the Kingdom of God are of fundamental importance in Mark's portrayal of Jesus. They sow some important seeds in our minds which will help us to understand the Gospel of Mark.

Icon representing the Baptism of Christ.

## What Kind of Text?

These opening fifteen verses of the Gospel according to Mark are a collection of different kinds of texts. The Gospel begins with a proclamation of faith that Jesus is both 'Christ' and 'Son of God'. There follows a quotation from the Jewish Scriptures, as Mark suggests that the 'Old Testament' is fulfilled for Christians by the coming of Jesus. As the story gets underway Mark provides a description of the person and ministry of John the Baptist. Two brief narratives about Jesus follow, his baptism and the story of the temptation of Jesus. These narratives are not simply stories, for they contain within them fundamental statements about the person and mission of Jesus, that we might call christological statements. We will explore these in the commentary. The final verses of our passage, verses 14 and 15, are Mark's introduction to the actual ministry of Jesus.

*The text we are considering contains two of the new mysteries of the Rosary which Pope John Paul II has set before us as the 'Luminous Mysteries'. These mysteries provide an opportunity for praying the Rosary while considering the actual ministry of Jesus. The first of these mysteries is the Baptism of Jesus, which is narrated in verses 9-11, and the third is the Proclamation of the Kingdom and of Conversion, which we find in verses 14-15. This is a clear demonstration of the importance of these opening verses of Mark.*

The text which we are studying is extremely rich because Mark is explaining the deeper significance of the coming of Jesus. Mark begins to explain straightaway what he wrote in verse 1 when he declared Jesus to be 'Christ' and 'Son of God'.

River Jordan, where Jesus was baptized by John the Baptist.

# Commentary: verse by verse reading

**v.1** What Mark gives us in the opening verse of his gospel is a kind of headline: 'The beginning of the good news of Jesus Christ, the Son of God'. We should remember that the 'good news' or 'gospel' was originally not something written down but something preached. St Paul, at the beginning of his Letter to the Romans, describes himself as 'a servant of Jesus Christ, set apart for the gospel of God' (*Romans* 1:1). His life's work was to travel around preaching the good news about Jesus. Mark is then recording something which had been proclaimed by the disciples of Jesus and which was only subsequently written down.

Jesus is given two titles, both of which have tremendous significance. The title 'Christ' is derived from the Greek word for 'anointed one' and is the equivalent of the Hebrew term 'Messiah'. Remember that the gospels are written in Greek, while the Jewish Scriptures are written down mostly in Hebrew. The Jewish Scriptures contain many references to the longed-for anointed one. This anointed one is sometimes referred to as 'Son of God', as when the prophet Nathan makes a promise to David and his descendants that they will be 'sons of God' (2 *Samuel* 7:14). Mark intends something more here. Jesus is not simply an anointed king, but the unique Son of God.

## The Jewish Scriptures

**vv.2-3** These verses contain a quotation which the author states is from the book of Isaiah. A search through the books of the prophets in the Old Testament reveals that this quotation is made up of Malachi 3:1 and Isaiah 40:3. The two texts have been fused together in Christian use. This is the first time we see the evangelist use the Old Testament in explaining what is being reported about Jesus. The first Christian preachers used the Old Testament and proclaimed that certain texts were being 'fulfilled' in Jesus. Both the texts in this quotation refer to a messenger sent by God to 'prepare the way'. These two texts from Jewish prophets prepare for the entry of John the Baptist.

*The name of Jesus is not unique to Jesus. The English name 'Jesus' reaches us from the Greek 'Iesous', but the original Hebrew form was 'Yehoshua' or 'Yeshua' for short. It meant 'Yahweh helps', but was often interpreted as 'Yahweh saves'. The same name belonged to Moses' successor Joshua, and to the writer of the Book of Ecclesiasticus, whose name we remember as 'Jesus, son of Sira'. Christians in Spanish-speaking countries still give the name 'Jesus' to their sons.*

# John the Baptist

**vv.4-5** John is presented as 'baptizer'. Regular ritual washings were common practice among the Jewish people, as we read in Mark 7:3-4. This baptism of repentance, on the other hand, appears unique to John the Baptist. It is understood to have provided the recipient with a once-only experience of turning back to God, of changing mind and heart (in Greek *metanoia*). The evangelist stresses that a great number of people were attracted by the preaching of John. He may perhaps be exaggerating when he says 'all the people of Jerusalem'.

**v.6** Mark's description of John's clothing is similar to that of the prophet Elijah in the Second Book of Kings 1:8. This is not mere coincidence. The prophet Malachi, whose words we read in v.2, says later in his book in 4:5 (3:23) that the messenger would be a new Elijah. The evangelist intends us to consider this prophecy to have been fulfilled with the coming of John the Baptist. The gospels often make connections between John and Elijah, as in Mark 9:13 and Luke 1:17. As far as his food was concerned, John seems to have lived on whatever was available in the wilderness.

**vv.7-8** Unlike Matthew and Luke (in *Matthew* 3:7-10 and *Luke* 3:7-14), Mark does not provide great detail about the preaching of the Baptist. He limits his account to John's words about the one who is to come. John declares that this person will be 'more powerful'. He senses that the Messiah will have to engage in a battle against evil. Furthermore, John stresses his own unworthiness in relation to the coming Messiah, who will baptise with a greater baptism, the baptism of the Holy Spirit. These words of John would have made very clear to the early Christians that Jesus was greater than John the Baptist, despite the fact that it was John who baptised Jesus.

Saint John the Baptist by Michelozzo
(1396-1472) c. 1450.

# The Baptism of Jesus

**v.9** Jesus now appears for the first time in the Gospel according to Mark, which is why we are told of his place of origin. Nazareth was a small village in the southern part of Galilee, lying fifteen miles to the west of the Sea of Galilee, and about twenty miles from the Mediterranean. Nazareth is never mentioned in the Jewish Scriptures.

Mark then tells us of the baptism of Jesus by John. It is an extraordinary act of humility, that Jesus, who is sinless, should undergo a 'baptism of repentance for the forgiveness of sins'. Mark shows us how Jesus stands in solidarity with sinners. Matthew's account of the baptism includes a short dialogue between Jesus and John, in which John, who has misgivings, is told by Jesus 'to fulfil all righteousness' (*Matthew* 3:14-15).

**v.10** In his vision Jesus sees the heavens opened, just as the prophet Ezekiel is able to see visions from God at the beginning of his book (*Ezekiel* 1:1). Jesus sees the Spirit, descending like a dove. Isaiah the prophet expected such a descent of the Spirit on the anointed one: 'The spirit of the Lord shall rest on him'. (*Isaiah* 11:2). Just as the prophets had visions of God to call them to preach, so Jesus is presented as having a vision at the beginning of his ministry.

**v.11** Jesus also hears a voice from heaven. These words of God are particularly important and are understood to be derived from Psalm 2, in which God declares to the anointed king 'You are my son!' (verse 7), and from Isaiah 42:1, in which God addresses his chosen servant as 'beloved'. The vision seen by Jesus and the voice heard by him demonstrate his identity as the Spirit-filled Messiah and servant of God.

*The Jewish historian Josephus, who wrote in the late first century AD, speaks of John the Baptist's ministry in the following terms:*

*John was a good man and commanded the Jews to practise virtue, by exercising justice towards one another and piety towards God, and to come together to baptism.*

*(Antiquities 18,116)*

*Christian writers have explored the reasons for the baptism of Jesus by John. St Bede, the scholarly monk of Jarrow, wrote a commentary on the Gospel of Mark about the year 700. Bede writes:*

*He was baptized that by being baptized himself he might show his approval of John's baptism, and that by sanctifying the waters of Jordan through the descent of the dove he might show the coming of the Holy Spirit in the washing of believers.*

*(Bede, Commentary on Mark)*

*The preface for the Feast of the Birth of John the Baptist reads:*

*He baptized Christ, the giver of baptism, in waters made holy by the one who was baptized.*

# The Temptation

**vv.12-13** Filled with the Spirit, Jesus is drawn into the wilderness, the place where evil spirits are thought to dwell. Mark tells us in a very brief account that Jesus encounters Satan. The name 'Satan', which means 'adversary', is given to an official in the court of God in the book of Job. The Satan has the role of an accuser or prosecutor. In time, Satan was identified with the serpent which, according to the story in the book of Genesis, tempted Adam and Eve in Eden (*Genesis* 3). Satan was considered to be the origin of temptation and of sin. It is therefore fitting that Jesus, the 'more powerful one' who is filled with the Spirit, should confront Satan.

What Jesus does is highly symbolic. Just as the people of Israel had spent forty years in the desert being tested (*Deuteronomy* 8:2), now Jesus is tested for forty days in the desert. Forty days was also the length of time spent in the wilderness by the prophet Elijah (1 *Kings* 19:8). That Jesus was with the wild beasts is more difficult to interpret and possibly alludes to the protection given by God in Psalm 91, which also refers to the assistance provided by angels for those who trust in God. When our text says that 'the angels waited on him' there may also be another allusion to Elijah, who received food from an angel for his desert journey (1 *Kings* 19:5-8).

*By the solemn forty days of Lent the Church unites herself each year to the mystery of Jesus in the desert.*

*(Catechism of the Catholic Church n.540)*

A rare combination of the Baptism and Temptation by Paolo Veronese (1528-1588)

# The Kingdom of God

**vv.14-15** Our final verses tell of the beginning of Jesus' ministry. Mark tells us that he proclaims 'the good news of God'. The first words of Jesus which Mark records are a type of summary of his preaching, a kind of manifesto. Jesus declares that 'the time', in Greek *kairos*, is fulfilled. The events which are about to unfold are the climax of a long period of waiting, and they are a special period of grace for the world. Jesus also declares that the 'kingdom of God' has come near. This idea is fundamental to the preaching of Jesus and refers to God's action in the world to confront evil and death, and to establish God's reign. Jesus will repeatedly speak of the kingdom in all three synoptic gospels (*Matthew*, *Mark* and *Luke*).

*The Second Vatican Council (1962-1965) has this to say about the Kingdom of God:*

*The Lord Jesus inaugurated his church by preaching the good news of the coming of the kingdom of God, promised over the ages in the Scriptures: 'The time is fulfilled, and the kingdom of God is at hand'. This kingdom shines out before humanity in the words, the works and the presence of Christ.*

*(Lumen Gentium n.5)*

*Today some commentators prefer to speak of 'the reign of God'. Both 'kingdom' and 'reign' refer to God's universal rule. God is the God of all peoples and of the universe.*

Christ the Light of The World. The statue dominates the skyline of Rio de Janeiro.

## The Word Lives On

The opening verses of the Gospel of Mark have provided fertile ground for the reflection of Christians for almost two-thousand years.

Matthew and Luke enrich Mark's account in various ways. Both give us more detail of the preaching of John the Baptist (*Matthew* 3 and *Luke* 3). Matthew and Luke also develop the baptism scene, and, when it comes to the temptation of Jesus, both report a dialogue between Jesus and Satan.

## In the Lectionary

The opening verses of Mark's gospel, with their focus on John the Baptist, are read on the 2nd Sunday of Advent in Year B. The narrative of the Baptism of Jesus is read in Year B on the final Sunday of the Christmas period, the Feast of the Baptism of the Lord. Jesus' initial proclamation of the Kingdom of God is heard in Year B on the 3rd Sunday in Ordinary Time.

*St Augustine of Hippo, one of the greatest fathers of the Latin Church (AD 354-430), writes this about Baptism:*

*Those who receive the baptism of Christ need not seek the baptism of John. Those who received the baptism of John did indeed seek the baptism of Christ... No baptism was necessary for Christ, but he freely received the baptism of a servant to draw us toward his baptism.*

*(Tractate on John)*

The Sabaeans, an ancient sect of Christians who believe John the Baptist is their prophet, perform mass baptisms after their Sunday service in Baghdad.

# Live the Word of God

**Listen again to the reading: Mark 1:1-15**

**What do you hear now?**

*Suggestions for reflection and prayer*

**What do you notice about Mark's presentation of Jesus?**

**Reflect on the words of St Jerome on this page, particularly the final sentence.**

**How might we as Christians of today witness more fully to the kingdom of God?**

**John the Baptist preached about the need to change.**

❖ Pray for openness to hear the gospel again with new understanding and a new heart.

**Jesus came as the Christ-Servant.**

❖ Pray for the grace to live as servants in imitation of Christ.

**Jesus proclaimed that the time had come.**

❖ Pray for all who preach the good news of the kingdom in word and deed.

## Reflect

*St Jerome (c.345-420), another of the great fathers of the Latin Church, wrote about John the Baptist as follows:*

*John the Baptist had a religious mother and his father was a priest. Yet neither his mother's affection nor his father's affluence could induce him to live in his parents' house at the risk of the world's temptations. So he lived in the desert. Seeking Christ with his eyes, he refused to look at anything else. ...*

*Later, the spiritual descendants of the prophets, who were the monks of the Old Testament, would build for themselves huts by the waters of Jordan and, forsaking the crowded cities, live in these on pottage and wild herbs. As long as you are at home make your cell your paradise, gather there the varied fruits of Scripture, let them be your favourite companions, and take its precepts to your heart.*

*(Letter to Rusticus)*

Marking time?
Making time?

# Miracles in Capernaum

# Hear the Word of God

## Read Mark 1: 21-34

21 They went to Capernaum; and when the sabbath came, he entered the synagogue and taught. 22 They were astounded at his teaching, for he taught them as one having authority, and not as the scribes.

23 Just then there was in their synagogue a man with an unclean spirit, 24 and he cried out, 'What have you to do with us, Jesus of Nazareth? Have you come to destroy us? I know who you are, the Holy One of God.'

25 But Jesus rebuked him, saying, 'Be silent, and come out of him!'

26 And the unclean spirit, convulsing him and crying with a loud voice, came out of him. 27 They were all amazed, and they kept on asking one another, 'What is this? A new teaching--with authority! He commands even the unclean spirits, and they obey him.' 28 At once his fame began to spread throughout the surrounding region of Galilee.

29 As soon as they left the synagogue, they entered the house of Simon and Andrew, with James and John. 30 Now Simon's mother-in-law was in bed with a fever, and they told him about her at once. 31 He came and took her by the hand and lifted her up. Then the fever left her, and she began to serve them.

32 That evening, at sundown, they brought to him all who were sick or possessed with demons. 33 And the whole city was gathered around the door. 34 And he cured many who were sick with various diseases, and cast out many demons; and he would not permit the demons to speak, because they knew him.

Facing page: Aerial view of Capernaum on the shores of the Sea of Galilee.
The grey roof is the modern church built over the traditional site of the house of St Peter.

# Understand the Word of God

**This session will explore:**

- ❖ a typical day in the ministry of Jesus
- ❖ the miracles of Jesus
- ❖ Jesus' outreach to those in need
- ❖ the message for today.

## Setting in the Gospel

The ministry of Jesus begins with teaching and healing. We hear of the healing by Jesus of a man described as having an unclean spirit and of the mother-in-law of Simon Peter. These are the first of the healings performed by Jesus in this, the earliest gospel.

Straight after the call of the first disciples to leave everything and follow Jesus, the evangelist gives us an account of a typical day in the ministry of Jesus in Galilee.

Ruins of the synagogue at Capernaum.

It is the sabbath (v.21). Jesus goes to the synagogue at Capernaum, where he teaches the people, and then immediately to the house of Simon Peter's mother-in-law (v.31). Several other healings take place that evening (vv.32-34). Then Mark tells us that Jesus is found praying in a lonely place in the early morning (vv.35-36).

# What Kind of Text?

We generally call texts like this one 'miracle stories', but the synoptic gospels use the Greek word *dynameis* (for example in *Mark* 6:2) when they refer to the healings of Jesus. The word really means 'acts of power' or 'mighty deeds'. Jesus heals by the power of God at work in him, confronting the power of evil which has taken hold of the sick. These stories of the mighty deeds of Jesus show that his mission is to heal and to challenge the evil which invades people's lives. In this way Jesus demonstrates the coming of the Kingdom of God, the triumph of God over all those things which undermine God's peace (*Mark* 1:15).

The perceived presence of an unclean spirit in the man in the synagogue is challenged and expelled, so that this particular healing may also be understood as an 'exorcism', the driving out of a devil. In ancient times it was common to understand all sickness as having some connection with an evil spirit or devil, which does not mean that the sick person has deserved the illness, or is wicked themselves. In Luke 13:16 Jesus says that Satan has made a woman a cripple for eighteen years. Jesus' healing of the man means that he will no longer be looked upon as 'unclean'. He is no longer excluded from the community.

Stories of healing tend to include a description of the plight of the sick person, the intervention of the healer, and the reaction of the onlookers. Such elements are found also in other ancient stories about healers. The healings of Jesus reveal the power of God. It is useful to recall what Jesus says of the man born blind in chapter 9 of John's gospel: he was born blind 'so that the works of God might be displayed in him' (*John* 9:3).

*In instructing people about the mystery of sin the Church acknowledges the power of evil. In the Rite of Christian Initiation of Adults, the scrutinies are rites for self-searching and repentance. They are celebrated to inspire in the elect a desire for purification and redemption by Christ. On the third Sunday of Lent, the rite of exorcism celebrates deliverance from sin and new strength in Christ.*

*(See RCIA 128-131)*

*The ministry of exorcism is recognised within the Church but exercised with caution. In particular the Church warns against any association of illness with evil spirits.*

*(See Catechism of the Catholic Church, 1673)*

# Commentary: verse by verse reading

*We know of the existence of an early church from the writings of the Christian pilgrim Egeria, who visited the Holy Land at the end of the fourth century:*

*At Capernaum the house of the Prince of the Apostles has become a church, but the walls of the house are still preserved. There is also the synagogue in which the Lord healed the possessed man. Access to the synagogue is by way of many steps.*

**v.21** Jesus and his disciples come to the town of Capernaum on the north-west shore of the Sea of Galilee. The Gospel of Matthew will tell us that Jesus chose the town of Capernaum as his base during his ministry of teaching and healing in the region of Galilee (*Matthew 4:13*). Excavations have taken place at Capernaum at the site of the synagogue, and at the site thought to be that of Peter's house. There is evidence that this latter site was a place of pilgrimage for Christians from early times.

A modern church has been built over the traditional site of Peter's house. Archaeologists uncovered the ruins of a 4th century Byzantine church, possibly the one Egeria visited.

# In the Synagogue

**v.22** Jesus is allowed to teach in the synagogue, as any Jewish male could. There would have been synagogues in the main towns in Jesus' day, and prayers were held in them every sabbath day. Mark later mentions Jesus' visit to the synagogue in Nazareth (6:2). Though Mark tells us that Jesus taught, we have no idea from Mark's gospel what Jesus taught. Mark in fact records very little of the teaching of Jesus, except in chapters 4 and 13, and we obtain far fuller accounts of the actual teaching of Jesus in the gospels of Matthew and Luke. The evangelist says that Jesus taught 'with authority', and the same phrase will return in v. 27 in order to stress this point. The teaching of Jesus is unlike that of the scribes, who were the experts on Jewish traditional teaching. Later on in Mark scribes will come down from Jerusalem to investigate and challenge the teaching of Jesus (3:22, 7:1). Along with the chief priests, scribes will be involved in plotting the death of Jesus (14:1).

**v.23** The man is described as having 'an unclean spirit'. This is difficult to interpret with certainty. Due to his condition and behaviour, people think the man is suffering from the presence of an unclean or evil spirit. Nowadays we would probably understand the man to be suffering from some kind of mental illness. From the evangelist's perspective the man is suffering from the evil influence of Satan, and Jesus is able to expel such influence from his life. The fundamental point is that Jesus is the one who is stronger than all the forces of evil in the world. This will be demonstrated in the dialogue which follows.

**v.24** The man cries out to Jesus: What do you want with us? As in the later story of the Gerasene demoniac (5:9), it is implied that there are several demons troubling the man. Once again, this is the contemporary understanding of such behaviour.

The words shouted by the man are very interesting. If we were to translate the Greek of Mark's gospel more literally we would read: 'What to us and to you?' This seems to make little sense until we discover an almost identical expression used in the Old Testament in one of the stories of the prophet Elijah. When the son of the widow of

Zarephath is struck ill and dies, the distraught mother cries out to the prophet: 'What to me and to you?' (1 *Kings* 17:18)

Just like the sick man in the synagogue at Capernaum, the widow is attempting to defend herself against the power of a prophet she perceives as harmful. Greek expressions in the gospels often show traces of Hebrew or Semitic ways of speaking. The widow of Zarephath uses defensive language to Elijah, just like the sick man in the synagogue who speaks to Jesus. The man also speaks of an approaching destruction and tries to claim power over Jesus by proclaiming his name and revealing his identity.

**vv.25-26** Jesus' command to the unclean spirit to be silent and to leave the man leads to convulsions and shrieking on the part of the sick man. There is a similar reaction when Jesus heals the epileptic boy in Mark 9:25-26. For the evangelist, both mental and physical sicknesses are healed powerfully simply by the command of Jesus, and the evil effect of Satan is removed.

*The works and words of Jesus manifest him as the Holy One of God.*

*(Catechism of the Catholic Church, 438)*

**v.27** The man is totally transformed and the people express their amazement: Here is a teaching which is new, and with authority behind it. Both the teaching and the powerful healing work of Jesus amaze them. The teaching of Jesus about the coming of the Kingdom (1:15) is confirmed by the mighty deeds of Jesus as his work begins. The authority of God is revealed in Jesus.

**v.28** The reputation of Jesus spreads throughout the region of Galilee. For Mark, Galilee is the place where the preaching of Jesus is welcomed, and where he is able to do his healing work largely unhindered.

The artist sets the event in the world he knows. The encounter between Jesus and the possessed man takes place on the balcony. Some of the crowd look up with interest but the life of the city goes on all around. Jesus would have experienced much the same situation.

Carpaccio's Healing of the Possessed Man (Accademia, Venice)

# In Peter's House

**v.29** Jesus goes from the public location of the synagogue of Capernaum to the privacy of the house of Simon and Andrew. Simon and Andrew were the first two disciples called earlier in the chapter, and James and John, the other two called from their fishing-boats, accompany them. For the present the first of the disciples is referred to as Simon, but Mark will inform his readers in 3:16 that Jesus gave to Simon the new name Peter, a tradition that is elaborately explained in Matthew's gospel (*Matthew* 16:18-19), and in the Gospel of John (*John* 1:42).

**v.30** Simon's house is the location for a second healing by Jesus, this time of Simon's mother-in-law, who has a fever. There is no mention of Simon's wife.

*St Bede in his commentary on the Gospel of Mark writes this about Simon's mother-in-law:*

*The health which is conferred at the command of the Lord returns at once entire, accompanied with such strength that she is able to minister to those of whose help she had before stood in need.*

**v.31** The healing this time takes place not with a word of command but by physical contact. As in the raising up of the epileptic boy in chapter 9 of the gospel (*Mark* 9:27), Jesus 'took her by the hand and raised her up'. The word used here for 'raising up' is striking. It is the same word which is used of Jesus' resurrection. In this way we see that the healing acts of Jesus point to the new life of the resurrection. The woman's complete recovery is demonstrated when she begins to serve them.

**v.32** The day comes to an end and evening comes. At this point, since it is the end of the sabbath, during which strenuous work was not allowed, people begin to carry to Jesus people who are ill and those who have evil spirits. The man in the synagogue and Simon's mother-in-law are not the only people healed by Jesus.

**v.33** Mark reports that the whole town was gathered at the door of Simon's house.

**v.34** This final verse stresses the large number of people healed of diseases and the large number of evil spirits driven out. The more detailed stories of Jesus' miracles simply provide examples of the healing action that Jesus performed for large numbers of unknown people. Different evangelists record different healings of Jesus. A further interesting point is that Jesus forbids the evil spirits to speak because they knew him. Jesus is reluctant to have news of his identity spread abroad, since easy popularity could well undermine his mission of preaching and healing.

## The Word Lives On

## In Matthew and Luke

This text of Mark's gospel was taken up by Luke, and can be found in Luke 4:31-41. Matthew's gospel does not report the healing of the possessed man in the synagogue. The false accusation that Jesus worked exorcisms by collaborating with Satan (*Mark* 3:22-29) may have led to such stories being treated with a certain reserve. John's gospel does not report any exorcisms at all.

Matthew does record the healing of Simon's mother-in-law and of the other sick people in Matthew 8:14-16. Furthermore, Matthew 8:17 sees the healing of the sick as fulfilment of words found in Isaiah 53:4.

## In the Lectionary

This text of Mark's gospel is found in Cycle B for the 4th and 5th Sundays in Ordinary Time, and in the Weekday Lectionary on Tuesday and Wednesday of Week 1.

*St Jerome writes:*

*May Christ come to our house and enter in and by his command cure the fever of our sins. Each one of us is sick with a fever. Whenever I give way to anger, I have a fever. There are as many fevers as there are faults and vices. Let us beg the apostles to intercede for us with Jesus, that he may come to us and touch our hand. If he does so, at once our fever is gone.*

*(Homilies on the Gospel of Mark 75)*

# Live the Word of God

**Listen again to the reading: Mark 1:21-34**

**What do you hear now?**
*Suggestions for reflection and prayer*

**Is there anything you find particularly striking about Jesus' activity in Capernaum?**

**Reflect on the words of Pope John Paul II on this page, that the suffering of others calls forth our love.**

**How might outreach to those in need become a more significant feature of our lives?**

*The world of human suffering calls forth the world of human love.*

*Pope John Paul II, Salvifici Doloris. n.29*

**Jesus reaches out to the man who is both sick and an outcast.**

❖ Pray for the grace to live in solidarity with those who suffer.

**Peter's mother-in-law, once she has been healed by Jesus, shows hospitality to her guest.**

❖ Pray for the gift of sensitive hospitality, gratitude and generosity.

**The healing work of Jesus is continued in the work of his disciples in the present day.**

❖ Pray for those who provide care for the sick and the victims of violence throughout the world, particularly in places where provision is scarce.

# Parables by the Sea

# Hear the Word of God

## Read Mark 4:1-20

¹ Again he began to teach beside the sea. Such a very large crowd gathered around him that he got into a boat on the sea and sat there, while the whole crowd was beside the sea on the land. ² He began to teach them many things in parables, and in his teaching he said to them:

³ 'Listen! A sower went out to sow. ⁴ And as he sowed, some seed fell on the path, and the birds came and ate it up.

⁵ Other seed fell on rocky ground, where it did not have much soil, and it sprang up quickly, since it had no depth of soil. ⁶ And when the sun rose, it was scorched; and since it had no root, it withered away.

⁷ Other seed fell among thorns, and the thorns grew up and choked it, and it yielded no grain.

⁸ Other seed fell into good soil and brought forth grain, growing up and increasing and yielding thirty and sixty and a hundredfold.'

⁹ And he said, 'Let anyone with ears to hear listen!'

¹⁰ When he was alone, those who were around him along with the twelve asked him about the parables. ¹¹ And he said to them, 'To you has been given the secret of the kingdom of God, but for those outside, everything comes in parables; ¹² in order that 'they may indeed look, but not perceive, and may indeed listen, but not understand; so that they may not turn again and be forgiven'.'

¹³ And he said to them, 'Do you not understand this parable? Then how will you understand all the parables?

¹⁴ The sower sows the word. ¹⁵ These are the ones on the path where the word is sown: when they hear, Satan immediately comes and takes away the word that is sown in them.

¹⁶ And these are the ones sown on rocky ground: when they hear the word, they immediately receive it with joy. ¹⁷ But they have no root, and endure only for a while; then, when trouble or persecution arises on account of the word, immediately they fall away.

¹⁸ And others are those sown among the thorns: these are the ones who hear the word, ¹⁹ but the cares of the world, and the lure of wealth, and the desire for other things come in and choke the word, and it yields nothing.

²⁰ And these are the ones sown on the good soil: they hear the word and accept it and bear fruit, thirty and sixty and a hundredfold.'

Facing page: The Parable of the Sower by Abel Grimer, (c. 1570-p.1619)

# Understand the Word of God

**This session will explore:**

❖ Mark's gathering together of the parables of Jesus

❖ the meaning of the parable of the sower

❖ the purpose of the parables

❖ the message for today.

The Parable of the Sower
James Tissot.

## Setting in the Gospel

Mark's account of Jesus' ministry in Galilee began with the call of the first disciples and the description of a day's ministry in the town of Capernaum, by the Sea of Galilee (*Mark* 1:21-39). In the early chapters of the Gospel, Mark describes some of the mighty deeds of Jesus, and also tells us of the first controversies between Jesus and the religious leaders. In 3:6 there is even a reference to plots to do away with Jesus. The teaching of Jesus has so far been only briefly reported. In chapter 4, however, Mark has assembled a collection of parables of Jesus

# What Kind of Text?

While Mark collects a whole series of parables in chapter 4, this is not the first occasion in his gospel where we hear reference to parables. In chapter 3 the scribes, who had come down from Jerusalem, questioned Jesus concerning the source of his power to heal. Mark reports that Jesus 'called them to him, and spoke to them in parables'. (3:23)

Jesus then challenges them by referring to a divided kingdom, a divided house, and a house which is plundered. He uses these very short stories to illustrate his point. This shows us right from the start that a parable is a story with a message. Technically, the Greek word *parabole* refers to placing two things alongside each other, comparing them, understanding a new thing better through seeing similarities with something already well known. Jesus' hearers know all about the sowing of seeds. That knowledge will help them to understand the coming of the Kingdom.

In the Jewish Scriptures the Hebrew word *mashal* covers a great variety of different texts. A *mashal* can be a proverb, such as those found in the Book of Proverbs, but it can also refer to longer parable-like texts, such as we find in Ezekiel 17. There is one very good example of a story-parable, told by the prophet Nathan in 2 Samuel 12. Just as Nathan challenges king David with the story of the poor man's ewe lamb, so Jesus will challenge people with his parables.

*The Catechism of the Catholic Church (n.546) has this to say on the parables and the Kingdom:*

*Jesus' invitation to enter his kingdom comes in the form of parables, a characteristic feature of his teaching. Through his parables he invites people to the feast of the kingdom, but he also asks for a radical choice: to gain the kingdom, one must give everything. Words are not enough, deeds are required. The parables are like mirrors for man: will he be hard soil or good earth for the word? What use has he made of the talents he has received? Jesus and the presence of the kingdom in this world are secretly at the heart of the parables. One must enter the kingdom, that is, become a disciple of Christ, in order to 'know the secrets of the kingdom of heaven'. For those who stay 'outside', everything remains enigmatic.*

# Commentary: verse by verse reading

## The Parable of the Sower

**v.1** Once more, Jesus is teaching by the Sea of Galilee. In chapter 3 Jesus had also met the crowds by the sea and told his disciples to have a boat ready for him because of the crowd (3:9). Here Mark speaks of a very large crowd. On this occasion Jesus actually boards a boat, sits down and teaches the crowd from the boat. We might compare this opening with the beginning of the Sermon on the Mount, when the evangelist Matthew has Jesus ascend the mountain and sit down before beginning to teach the crowds (*Matthew* 5:1). There is a similar, rather solemn tone to the opening of this major discourse of Jesus in the Gospel of Mark. Quite apart from sitting down in order to teach, sitting down would have helped balance the boat.

**v.2** Mark again tells us that Jesus began his teaching, and that he taught many things in parables. Mark uses the Greek word *didache*, which means 'teaching'. The word *didache* will be used later in the New Testament to refer to the teaching of the apostles of Jesus, the foundation of the teaching of the Church (*Acts* 2:42).

St John Chrysostom, bishop of Constantinople in the 4th century and renowned for his preaching, says this about God's sowing:

*As the sower fairly and indiscriminately disperses seed broadly over all his field, so does God offer gifts to all, making no distinction between rich and poor, wise and foolish, lazy or diligent, brave or cowardly.*

(Homily 44.5.1)

**v.3** Jesus uses simple stories to claim the attention of his hearers. The parables refer to things familiar to the people of rural Galilee, activities concerned with farming and agriculture, with fishing in the Sea of Galilee, as well as domestic and social concerns.

**v.4** The parables of Jesus sometimes contain improbable details, which we might not notice due to our familiarity with the story. In the parable of the lost sheep (*Matthew* 18:12), we might ask how usual it would be to leave the ninety-nine sheep without protection in the wilderness to go and search for just one. In the parable of the sower we are told that the sower scatters the seed in places where it is unlikely to grow, such as on the path and on the rocks. These unlikely details illustrate the extraordinary generosity with which the seed is scattered, pointing to the abundance of God's generosity in sending out the word.

It is thought that the sower would have sown the seed 'broadcast' once the land had been ploughed with the help of oxen or asses. We read in 1 Kings 19:19 that the prophet Elisha was called as a disciple by the prophet Elijah while he was ploughing with a yoke of oxen. Iron ploughshares have been discovered in Israel, which date to ancient times.

Wheat was the most important crop, as it was the staple food, and barley was also grown. The main sowing took place in the autumn and the harvest in the spring.

'Listen! A sower went out to sow.'

The Sower: c.1200 by Benedetto Antelami, (c.1150-1230)

**vv.5-6** It was often necessary to clear the land of rocks and stones in order to cultivate crops. The land in Galilee was more fertile than in other parts of Palestine, but rocky ground was common. The parable shows an awareness of the problems of producing wheat from such ground.

**v.7** Sowing among thorns again illustrates the abundant generosity of the sower.

**v.8** Among the stories of the patriarchs of Israel in the book of Genesis we read the following about Abraham's son, Isaac: 'Isaac sowed seed in that land, and in the same year reaped a hundredfold. The Lord blessed him.' (*Genesis* 26:12) Isaac's abundant harvest in the land of the king of Gerar, to which he had travelled due to famine, is attributed to the special blessing of the Lord. In the parable of the sower the amounts given are also exceptional. A normal yield from a harvest would have provided far less. Once again, the parable presents an unusual situation in order to stress God's great generosity.

**v.9** Jesus ends the parable as he began it, with an appeal to listen. The saying found here is repeated later in the chapter (4:23) and is found in the other gospels too (e.g. *Matthew* 11:15 *Luke* 14:35). In Mark 8:18 Jesus will challenge the disciples with the words 'Do you have ears, and fail to hear?'

# The Secret of the Kingdom

**v.10**  The evangelist now presents Jesus in the company of 'those around him' and 'the twelve'. We cannot be sure to whom Mark is referring, but it would seem to be those who were close to Jesus and went with him on his travels. Later, Mark refers to the women who followed Jesus providing for him in Galilee (*Mark* 15:41). It seems that Jesus was accompanied by more people than the twelve he had chosen.

**v.11**  The close followers question Jesus about the parables, and the answer Jesus gives is difficult to interpret. 'To you has been given the secret of the kingdom of God,' says Jesus, 'but for those outside everything comes in parables.' Jesus' ministry, even in these early chapters, and increasingly so as he makes his way towards Jerusalem, has already incited opposition. There are those who are unwilling to listen, those who refuse to believe, those in whose lives the seed will not grow to fruition. They may be entertained by the stories Jesus tells, but they are not open to deeper understanding. When Jesus speaks of the 'secret of the kingdom of God', the evangelist uses the Greek word *mysterion,* sometimes translated as 'mystery'. The mystery is available to all, but all have the freedom to reject it.

*In the Letter to the Ephesians we read about the mystery hidden and now made known. It is that all peoples are called to be fellow-heirs with the Jewish people, sharing in the promise made by Christ Jesus in the gospel (Ephesians 3:1-6).*

**v.12**  More difficult to understand are the words of Scripture which Jesus quotes and adapts to his situation. They are from the narrative of the calling of the prophet Isaiah found in Isaiah chapter 6. The difficulties Isaiah will have in his preaching are foreseen in the words of God that people will look and not perceive, listen and not understand. The same phrases are applied by Jesus to the reaction to his own preaching. These words do not mean that Jesus intends people to reject his message, but that he foresaw that some would do so. Despite his encouragement to listen, he is aware that some people will not.

# Understanding the Parable

**v.13** Jesus is aware of the slowness of the disciples to understand the deeper significance of the parables. Jesus' story of the sower is more than an entertaining story about life in rural Galilee. It has a deeper meaning to convey. Jesus seems to pick up the uncertainty of the disciples. Have they understood correctly? Mark is very honest throughout his gospel in reporting the difficulties of the disciples and their slowness to understand.

**v.14** The word of God is compared to a seed sown by a sower. In the book of the prophet Isaiah the word of God is compared to the rain and snow which water the earth and bring fruitfulness (*Isaiah* 55:10-11). Comparing the word to a seed stresses the growth which should follow reception of the gospel, and which is fundamental to the faith of communities and individuals.

**v.15** In what is technically known as an allegorical interpretation, Jesus takes the details of the story one by one and relates them to the sowing of the word of God. Another allegorical interpretation is found when the parable of the darnel in the field in Matthew 13:24-30 is explained in 13:36-43. The seeds sown on the path represent people who allow Satan and the power of evil to frustrate the growth of the word in their lives. Even Peter, who proclaims his faith in Jesus in Mark 8:29, will be called 'Satan' by Jesus in Mark 8:33, when he questions Jesus' commitment to the way of suffering and death.

**vv.16-17** Those on rocky ground receive the word at first with joy, but this initial enthusiasm for Christ and the gospel is tested by difficulties. The reason why they endure only for a while is that they begin to experience 'trouble or persecution on account of the word'. Jesus often speaks of the expected suffering of his followers, even when assuring them of the rewards of discipleship (10:29-30).

Some disciple 'fall away'. The Greek word is *skandalizontai*, which can also be translated as 'stumble', and more literally as 'are scandalised'. It means that trouble and persecution become an insurmountable obstacle to their faith. They are scandalised by persecution. Jesus foresees in Gethsemane that his disciples will fall away and be scandalised (14:27). The prospect of suffering punishment and death for being his disciples will become an obstacle for their faith and will temporarily undermine their commitment to Jesus.

**vv.18-19** Other seeds fall among thorns. These people hear the word, but the growth of the word is choked by worldly cares, wealth, and the desire for other things. The rich young man who meets Jesus in Mark 10:17 cannot deepen his discipleship due to his great wealth (10:22). 'Desire for other things' is a deliberately vague expression covering all other worldly attractions, which, once the word of the gospel has been heard, may choke the word, seriously weakening the commitment of the believer and growth in discipleship.

**v.20** Finally, the explanation of the parable considers those who bring forth a rich harvest, with extraordinary yields. These people not only hear the word, but also welcome it. Listening to the word is simply the first stage. The word needs fertile ground in the hearts of believers.

*St Augustine of Hippo gives this advice:*

*Work diligently the soil while you may.*

*Break up your fallow with the plough.*

*Cast away the stones from your field and dig out the thorns.*

*Be unwilling to have a 'hard heart', such as makes the Word of God of no effect.*

*Be unwilling to have a 'thin layer of soil', in which the root of divine love can find no depth in which to enter.*

*Be unwilling to 'choke the good seed' by the cares and the lusts of this life, when it is being scattered for your good.*

*When God is the sower and we are the ground, we are called to work to be good ground.*

*(Sermons on New Testament Lessons 73.3)*

*At this spot by the sea of Galilee land and sea form a natural amphitheatre. Someone at the shoreline or in a boat, speaking in a normal voice, would be completely audible to the people sitting on the rocks. This spot is called the Cove of the Sower.*

## The Word Lives On

The parable of the Sower, since it is found in all three synoptic gospels and considers the basic issue of hearing the word, has achieved a special status among the parables. It is the first parable in the collection which Mark puts together in chapter 4 of his gospel. Matthew has a similar collection of parables in chapter 13, and also begins the collection with the Sower and its interpretation. Luke reports the parable of the Sower in chapter 8 of his gospel, following it only with the short parable of the lamp.

## In the Lectionary

Mark's version of the Sower is read each year on Wednesday of the third week in Ordinary Time. Matthew's version (*Matthew* 13:1-23) is read on the 15th Sunday in Ordinary Time, Year A.

# Live the Word of God

**Listen again to the reading: Mark 4:1-20**

**What do you hear now?**

*Suggestions for reflection and prayer*

**What message of encouragement do you consider the parable of the Sower might have for us today?**

**Reflect on the words of St. Augustine at the end of the commentary.**

**What might working to be 'good ground' require?**

**The abundant generosity of God is repeatedly emphasised in the parable.**

- ❖ Pray for the grace to receive the word gratefully, and to allow it to produce a rich harvest.

**Discipleship may lead to persecution.**

- ❖ Pray for all who experience trouble or persecution, that they may find the strength to persevere.

**The thorns choke the word.**

- ❖ Pray for all who recognise that the desires of this world do not bring true happiness, that they may grow in right judgement.

# Two Great Miracles

# Hear the Word of God

## Read Mark 6:35-52

[35] When it grew late, his disciples came to him and said, 'This is a deserted place, and the hour is now very late; [36] send them away so that they may go into the surrounding country and villages and buy something for themselves to eat.'

[37] But he answered them, 'You give them something to eat.' They said to him, 'Are we to go and buy two hundred denarii worth of bread, and give it to them to eat?'

[38] And he said to them, 'How many loaves have you? Go and see.' When they had found out, they said, 'Five, and two fish.'

[39] Then he ordered them to get all the people to sit down in groups on the green grass. [40] So they sat down in groups of hundreds and of fifties.

[41] Taking the five loaves and the two fish, he looked up to heaven, and blessed and broke the loaves, and gave them to his disciples to set before the people; and he divided the two fish among them all.

[42] And all ate and were filled; [43] and they took up twelve baskets full of broken pieces and of the fish. [44] Those who had eaten the loaves numbered five thousand men.

[45] Immediately he made his disciples get into the boat and go on ahead to the other side, to Bethsaida, while he dismissed the crowd. [46] After saying farewell to them, he went up on the mountain to pray.

[47] When evening came, the boat was out on the sea, and he was alone on the land. [48] When he saw that they were straining at the oars against an adverse wind, he came towards them early in the morning, walking on the sea. He intended to pass them by. [49] But when they saw him walking on the sea, they thought it was a ghost and cried out; [50] for they all saw him and were terrified. But immediately he spoke to them and said, 'Take heart, it is I; do not be afraid.'

[51] Then he got into the boat with them and the wind ceased. And they were utterly astounded, [52] for they did not understand about the loaves, but their hearts were hardened.

Facing page: Christ Feeds the Five Thousand by Italian School, (15th Century)
Christ Walking on the Waves, from an illuminated copy of 'Meditations on the Llife of Christ' by St Bonaventure.

# Understand the Word of God

**This session will explore:**

- ❖ the two miracles of the multiplication of the loaves and the walking on the water
- ❖ the prominence of these two miracles in the gospel tradition
- ❖ what these miracles tell us about Jesus
- ❖ the message for today.

## Setting in the Gospel

Mark's account of the ministry of Jesus in Galilee progresses. After the collection of parables in chapter 4, Mark provides a series of miracle stories in chapter 5. The account of Jesus' visit to Nazareth in 6:1-6 is followed by the sending out of the twelve disciples to preach repentance and heal people (6:7-13), and the report of the death of John the Baptist (6:14-29). We are then told that the disciples rejoin Jesus and, despite their efforts to seek rest for a while, great crowds gather once again so that Jesus shows compassion and teaches them (6:34).

The multiplication of the loaves, known also as the feeding of the five thousand, and the walking on the water are closely tied to each other. The same juxtaposition of these two miracles is found in Matthew chapter 14 and John chapter 6. Luke reports the multiplication of the loaves in chapter 9 of his gospel, but shows no knowledge of the walking on the water.

The importance and popularity of the story of the loaves is emphasised by the fact that a further multiplication of loaves, a feeding of four thousand people, is found in Mark 8:1-10, with a parallel account in Matthew 15:32-39.

# What Kind of Text?

We are already familiar with the healing miracles of Mark, to which the evangelist refers with the Greek word *dynameis*, literally meaning 'acts of power'. Jesus works such deeds to heal people, to demonstrate the compassionate love of God, and above all to announce the approach of the kingdom of God, in which evil and pain are to be conquered.

The two miracles we are reading now are not accounts of healing. By feeding the multitude Jesus comes to the assistance of the hungry people, but the walking on the water puts very little emphasis on what Jesus does for the disciples, since verse 51 simply says 'he got into the boat with them and the wind ceased'.

What these two miracles have in common is their focus on Jesus. In the book of Exodus God provides for the people in the wilderness by giving them manna and quails to eat (*Exodus* 16). God is shown, also, to have control over the sea in the story of the escape of the Israelites from Egypt in Exodus 14. These gospel stories demonstrate that Jesus displays both the loving concern and the power of God.

Such stories are technically referred to as 'epiphanies'. Just as the feast of the Epiphany celebrates the manifestation of Jesus as saviour of all peoples, so these stories reveal the divine qualities of Jesus. In fact, all miracle stories have an element of 'epiphany' about them, for, whenever Jesus heals people, he reveals his divine power.

Another text from the Jewish Scriptures is relevant here: 2 Kings 4:42-44. In this passage the prophet Elisha feeds one hundred people with twenty barley loaves and fresh ears of grain. At the end of the story it is narrated that 'they had some left'. Clearly, this miracle demonstrates that Elisha has particular God-given powers. The epiphany-miracles in the gospels proclaim not only that Jesus has similar powers, but that he is as God is. The epiphanies point to the divinity of Jesus.

*A man came from Baal-shalishah, bringing food from the first fruits to the man of God: twenty loaves of barley and fresh ears of grain in his sack. Elisha said, 'Give it to the people and let them eat.' But his servant said, 'How can I set this before a hundred people?' So he repeated, 'Give it to the people and let them eat, for thus says the Lord, 'They shall eat and have some left'.' He set it before them, they ate, and had some left, according to the word of the Lord.*

*(2 Kings 4:42-44. )*

# Commentary: verse by verse reading

## The Multiplication of the Loaves

**v.35** Mark stated in verse 31 that so many people were seeking Jesus that the disciples hardly had time to eat. Despite the efforts of Jesus to find some peace and quiet with the disciples, they were besieged by even larger crowds and Jesus taught them 'many things' (verse 34). Now the disciples are concerned that the crowds are hungry.

**v.36** The disciples' rather abrupt 'Send them away!' shows something of the frustration of the disciples at having no rest.

**v.37** There is a clear contrast between the attitude of the disciples and the tireless concern of Jesus for the people. Jesus, who has taught the crowds at some length, will now provide them with food. The disciples are again portrayed by Mark as having little understanding of what Jesus is about. They refer to needing 'two hundred denarii' to buy bread for such a crowd. Their rather indignant question is omitted in the versions of the story found in Matthew 14 and Luke 9.

**v.38** The loaves would have been round and flat, about 20 cm. in diameter. Proximity to the sea of Galilee explains the availability of fish, which had no doubt been dried.

**vv.39-40** Mark's deliberate reference to 'green' grass indicates that it is springtime. By late May the grass is no longer green due to the increasing heat of the summer. That the miracle took place at this time is borne out by the account of the miracle in John 6, where the evangelist says that the Passover was near. The curious detail that the crowd sat down 'in groups of hundreds and of fifties' is possibly a result of the elaboration of the account by the story-teller, but there may be an allusion to the organisation of the people by Moses in groups of 'thousands, hundreds, fifties and tens' (*Exodus* 18:21).

*'Are we to go and buy two hundred denarii worth of bread?'*

*The parable of the labourers in the vineyard in Matthew chapter 20 tells us that one denarius was the wage for a day's work. The gospel references to coins of various types reflect the complicated history of Israel in the centuries around the time of Christ. The denarius is originally a Roman coin. We also find references to the Greek drachma and to other coins. The poor widow in Mark 12:42 makes an offering of 'two small copper coins, which are worth a penny'. The Greek text speaks of 'two lepta which are one kodrantes'. The lepton was the smallest coin in circulation in Palestine. The kodrantes was the smallest Roman coin, known in Latin as the quadrans. Two lepta would be about one 64th of a denarius.*

**v.41** The most remarkable feature of this verse is the close similarity between the actions of Jesus here and what he does at the Last Supper. In Mark 14:22 Jesus 'takes' bread, 'blesses' it, 'breaks' it and 'gives' it. The multiplication of the loaves is recorded in such a way that we cannot fail to make a connection with Jesus' gift of himself at the Last Supper.

**vv.42-44** Whereas the story of Elisha's miracle in 2 Kings 4:42-44 speaks of some food left over, the amount left over here is far more than the amount available at the start. This feature of the story stresses the magnitude of the miracle, as does the final note that 'five thousand men' had eaten. Matthew's account will clarify that this is an estimate which does not include the women and children present (*Matthew 14:21*). While Elisha had fed one hundred men with twenty loaves, Jesus feeds five thousand with five. The story proclaims in this way the superiority of Jesus.

*The traditional Jewish blessing of the bread at the passover meal reads:*

*Blessed are you, Lord our God, king of the universe, who bring forth bread from the earth!*

*The ancient Christian pilgrim Egeria visited the site in the fourth century and wrote:*

*Not far from Capernaum can be seen some stone steps on which the Lord stood. In the same place by the sea there is a grassy meadow with plenty of hay and many palm trees. Nearby are seven springs which produce water in abundance. It was in this field that the Lord fed the people with five loaves and two fish.*

*When the traditional location of this miracle, by the shore of the sea of Galilee at Tabgha, was excavated in the 1930s, the foundations of a large ancient basilica were discovered. The basilica has since been rebuilt. In the church pilgrims can see a mosaic of a basket of loaves and two fish, which dates back to the fifth or sixth century AD.*

Mosaic at the Church of the Multiplication of the Loaves, Galilee.

# The Walking on the Water

**v.45** Jesus' plan to provide rest for the disciples has failed. The evangelist states that Jesus 'made' or 'forced' his disciples to leave. This curious expression may be explained by referring again to the parallel story in John's gospel. After the multiplication of the loaves the evangelist says, 'When Jesus realized that they were about to come and take him by force to make him king, he withdrew again to the mountain by himself.' (*John* 6:15) It is quite possible that messianic enthusiasm was stirred up by the miracle and that Jesus was afraid that the crowds had got the wrong idea about his mission. This may explain why he forces the disciples to leave. Their destination is the town of Bethsaida on the north-eastern shore of the sea of Galilee.

**vv.46-47** Jesus is at prayer until evening. There is a tension here with the earlier statement that it was 'already very late' (6:35). Mark seems to have placed together two stories of miracles as if they had happened on the same day. This is a good example of the evangelist's editing of the material for catechetical purposes. He wants us to read these two miracles together.

**v.48** The story now becomes rather mysterious. Jesus is aware that the disciples are in trouble. He walks towards them 'early in the morning'. The original Greek reads 'in the fourth watch', a reference which employs the Roman way of reckoning the time between 3 a.m. and 6 a.m. The story tells us that Jesus has divine power, for Jesus is able to do what God is shown doing in the Jewish Scriptures. In the book of Job (9:8) we read: 'God alone stretched out the heavens, and trampled the waves of the Sea.' In 38:16 God challenges Job with the question: 'Have you entered into the springs of the sea, or walked in the recesses of the deep?' What Job cannot do, God can do. The gospel proclaims that Jesus has the power that God has.

Throughout the centuries people have asked what really happened. It is a question we can never answer adequately. The essential point is to understand that in these two miracle stories Jesus reveals the loving care and the power of God. They raise the question: Who then is Jesus?

*The town of Bethsaida was rebuilt by Philip, one of the sons of Herod the Great. He dedicated the town to Julia, the daughter of the emperor Augustus, and renamed it 'Bethsaida Julias'. The Gospel of John informs us that Peter, his brother Andrew, and the disciple called Philip were all from Bethsaida (John 1:44).*

*St Augustine of Hippo writes:*

*The fourth watch of the night marks the end of the night. One watch consists of three hours. This means that at the end of the world the Lord will come to the rescue, and he will be seen walking on the water. Although this ship is tossed by the storms of temptation, it sees the glorified Lord walking upon all the billows of the sea – that is, upon all the powers of this world.*

*(Sermon 75.7)*

**vv.49-50** The reaction of the disciples is predictably one of terror, but Jesus' words reassure them. The words 'It is I' translate the Greek *ego eimi*. These words remind us of God's words to Moses from the burning bush in the story in Exodus 3:14, 'I am who I am.' Just as the revelation of the power of God terrified Moses, the revelation of the power of Jesus terrifies the disciples. Jesus calms the fears of the disciples.

**vv.51-52** As Jesus enters the boat the wind ceases. This recalls the earlier miracle of the stilling of the storm in Mark 4. The evangelist ends the story by telling us of the confusion of the disciples, and adds rather curiously that they did not understand about the loaves. For Mark, the disciples fail to see the deeper significance of either miracle. They are not yet able to see how their experiences of Jesus reveal his divine power. The reason Mark gives is that their hearts, understood as the seat of understanding and reflection rather than of emotion, were hardened. When Jesus is about to heal the man with the withered hand in Mark 3:5 the evangelist tells us that Jesus is grieved at the 'hardness of heart' of the synagogue elders. Mark thus provides rather a negative account of the disciples' reaction to these two miracles, blaming them for their lack of understanding.

**Psalm 77:16-20**

*When the waters saw you, O God, when the waters saw you, they were afraid; the very deep trembled.*

*The clouds poured out water; the skies thundered; your arrows flashed on every side.*

*The crash of your thunder was in the whirlwind; your lightnings lit up the world; the earth trembled and shook.*

*Your way was through the sea, your path, through the mighty waters; yet your footprints were unseen.*

*You led your people like a flock by the hand of Moses and Aaron.*

## The Word Lives On

While Matthew and Luke give rather similar accounts of the feeding of the five thousand, Matthew includes two remarkable new features in his story of the walking on the water.

In Matthew 14:28-31 the evangelist reports that Peter too walks on the water but that he begins to sink when he feels the strength of the wind. Jesus reprimands Peter with the words: 'You of little faith, why did you doubt?' Matthew thus develops the story by including this encouragement to faith in difficult circumstances.

A further change in Matthew's account is found in the reaction of the disciples once Jesus has entered the boat. We read: 'Those in the boat worshipped him, saying: Truly you are the Son of God.' (*Matthew 14:33*)

The disciples are portrayed in a positive way. Matthew testifies to the faith which they would later proclaim and for which they would die.

## In the Lectionary

Mark's accounts of the miracle of the loaves and the walking on the water are never read at Sunday Mass. This is because the versions of these stories in the sixth chapter of John supplant the Gospel of Mark for several Sundays of Ordinary Time in Year B. Mark's accounts are read at Mass on the days between the Epiphany and the Baptism of the Lord.

Christ convinces Peter that he can walk on water by Italian School, (15th century)

# Live the Word of God

**Listen again to the reading: Mark 6:35-52**

**What do you hear now?**

*Suggestions for reflection and prayer*

**What do you find most memorable in the stories of these two miracles?**

**Reflect how Jesus offers nourishment to the crowd and encouragement amid danger to the disciples.**

**How might these stories still speak to us today?**

**In the Eucharist Christ comes 'in word and sacrament to strengthen us in holiness'.**

❖ Pray for the grace to value both word and sacrament as gifts of the Lord to his church.

**God crowns human generosity.**

❖ Pray for the generosity to share whatever we have with those around us, even when it costs.

**The walking on the water teaches us to trust in the mysterious presence of Christ amid the struggles and storms of our lives.**

❖ Pray for courage, and for trust in the goodness of God, despite the troubles and tragedies we see around us constantly.

**Hardness of heart, a reluctance to go deeper, being satisfied with what is superficial: all these undermine our growth in faith.**

❖ Pray for openness of spirit, and for a yearning to discover what is still hidden from our sight.

## Reflect

*Jesus provides nourishment for the crowd both by his teaching and by giving them food. Both are precious gifts not to be wasted.*

*God's gifts are to be shared. Jesus first invites the disciples to share what they have before providing what they need.*

# Eyes are Opened

# Hear the Word of God

## Read Mark 8:22-38

22 They came to Bethsaida. Some people brought a blind man to him and begged him to touch him. 23 He took the blind man by the hand and led him out of the village; and when he had put saliva on his eyes and laid his hands on him, he asked him, 'Can you see anything?'

24 And the man looked up and said, 'I can see people, but they look like trees, walking.'

25 Then Jesus laid his hands on his eyes again; and he looked intently and his sight was restored, and he saw everything clearly. 26 Then he sent him away to his home, saying, 'Do not even go into the village.'

27 Jesus went on with his disciples to the villages of Caesarea Philippi; and on the way he asked his disciples, 'Who do people say that I am?'

28 And they answered him, 'John the Baptist; and others, Elijah; and still others, one of the prophets.'

29 He asked them, 'But who do you say that I am?' Peter answered him, 'You are the Messiah.' 30 And he sternly ordered them not to tell anyone about him.

31 Then he began to teach them that the Son of Man must undergo great suffering, and be rejected by the elders, the chief priests, and the scribes, and be killed, and after three days rise again.

32 He said all this quite openly. And Peter took him aside and began to rebuke him. 33 But turning and looking at his disciples, he rebuked Peter and said, 'Get behind me, Satan! For you are setting your mind not on divine things but on human things.'

34 He called the crowd with his disciples, and said to them, 'If any want to become my followers, let them deny themselves and take up their cross and follow me. 35 For those who want to save their life will lose it, and those who lose their life for my sake, and for the sake of the gospel, will save it. 36 For what will it profit them to gain the whole world and forfeit their life? 37 Indeed, what can they give in return for their life? 38 Those who are ashamed of me and of my words in this adulterous and sinful generation, of them the Son of Man will also be ashamed when he comes in the glory of his Father with the holy angels.'

Facing page: Sculpture Relief depicting Christ Healing the Blind Man

# Understand the Word of God

**This session will explore:**

- ❖ the opening of the eyes of the blind man at Bethsaida and the growing faith of Peter and the disciples
- ❖ Peter's declaration of faith in Jesus
- ❖ what it means for Jesus to be the Messiah
- ❖ the cross of Jesus and the cross of Christians
- ❖ the message for today.

## Setting in the Gospel

With this text we reach the half-way point in the Gospel of Mark. So far the evangelist has provided an account of the ministry of Jesus in Galilee, a ministry of teaching and miracles. There has been some opposition to Jesus, as in his home town (*Mark* 6:1-6), but generally the words and actions of Jesus have been welcomed by the people.

Our text begins with the healing of the blind man at Bethsaida, a physical enlightenment. The focus then moves to the enlightenment of the minds of Peter and the disciples. When Peter declares that Jesus is the Christ, the Messiah, we reach something of a climax in the gospel, but, as the dialogue between Jesus and Peter continues, a new element is introduced. Jesus tells the disciples that he is destined to suffer and die, and to be raised up.

These new themes will dominate the Gospel of Mark from now on, and the disciples will struggle to accept Jesus' coming suffering and his warning that they too will suffer.

The dialogue between Jesus and the disciples takes place near Caesarea Philippi, the most northerly location in the gospel story. From here Jesus will journey south to Jerusalem and will enter, for the first time in this gospel, the city which is the religious and political capital of the Jews. The geographical journey is also a spiritual one, as the disciples of Jesus are confronted with the challenge of the cross.

# What Kind of Text?

We have already explored some of the miracles of Mark, to which the evangelist refers with the Greek term *dynameis*, meaning 'acts of power'. By his acts of healing Jesus announces the arrival of the kingdom of God, in which evil and pain are to be conquered. They may be seen also as signs that the Messiah has come.

The healing of the blind man at Bethsaida in Mark 8:22-26 is reported only in this gospel. In this respect it is like the healing of the deaf and dumb man in Mark 7:31-37. Both miracles take place in private and in both Jesus uses saliva in his healing treatment. It was perhaps the presence of the details of the cure that led to their omission by later evangelists. Mark reports another healing of a blind man, the one called Bartimaeus, who is healed by Jesus in the vicinity of Jericho simply by a word of command (*Mark* 10:46-52).

The miracle story is followed by a dialogue between Jesus and the disciples concerning his identity and his suffering. The text concludes with the teaching of Jesus to 'the crowd with his disciples' about the suffering involved in discipleship.

*We read in the book of Isaiah:*

*Then the eyes of the blind shall be opened,*

*and the ears of the deaf unstopped; then the lame shall leap like a deer, and the tongue of the speechless sing for joy.*

*For waters shall break forth in the wilderness, and streams in the desert;*

*the burning sand shall become a pool,*

*and the thirsty ground springs of water;*

*the haunt of jackals shall become a swamp,*

*the grass shall become reeds and rushes.*

*(Isaiah 35:5-7)*

Christ healing the blind man by El Greco (1541-1614). Some of the bystanders see what Christ does and respond in amazement; others seem unaware what is happening.

# Commentary: verse by verse reading

## The Healing of the Blind man at Bethsaida

**v.22** Jesus and the disciples are once again in Bethsaida, a town which has already been mentioned in Mark 6:45. The blind man is led to Jesus by some people who trust that simply at the touch of Jesus the blindness can be healed. It was significantly by touch that Jesus had healed the leper in Mark 1:41, and in Mark 5:28-31 the sick woman was healed simply by touching the garments of Jesus.

*Such extraordinary power of healing is reported also in the Acts of the Apostles:*

*They even carried out the sick into the streets, and laid them on cots and mats, in order that Peter's shadow might fall on some of them as he came by. A great number of people would also gather from the towns around Jerusalem, bringing the sick and those tormented by unclean spirits, and they were all cured.*

*(Acts 5:15-16)*

**v.23** The text states that Jesus 'took the blind man by the hand'. The one who had to be led to Jesus is now led by Jesus. Bethsaida is referred to here with the Greek word meaning 'village'. In fact, having been rebuilt in recent times, it seems to have been a town or city. Luke calls it a city in Luke 9:10. As in Mark 7:33 Jesus takes the man away in private, possibly in order to avoid unwanted attention or publicity. The use of spittle in the working of miracles is widely attested in the ancient world. Jesus also lays his hands on the man.

**v.24** The man gradually begins to see. His curious remark that he sees people walking like trees suggests some confusion and the gradualness of sight being restored.

**v.25** Jesus again lays hands on the man. The gradual healing by repeated touching of the blind man shows the compassion and care of Jesus. The healing is not rushed. Jesus knows that people need time to heal. The man who had 'looked up' in verse 24 now 'looks intently'. Being restored to health he 'sees everything clearly'. The original Greek text uses different forms of the basic word *blepein*, which means 'to look'. In this way the evangelist lays heavy emphasis on the restoration of the gift of sight.

**v.26** The final verse seems rather stern. Jesus' command is probably intended to avoid a commotion and undesired popular acclaim at the healing.

# Peter's Profession of Faith

**v.27** Jesus comes to the region of Caesarea Philippi, a northern town which had recently been rebuilt by Philip, the son of Herod the Great, and dedicated to the Roman emperor Augustus. Hence the name 'Caesarea of Philip'. As the journey south to Jerusalem begins, Jesus asks the disciples what people are saying about him.

**v.28** The answer of the disciples echoes what was stated in Mark 6:14-15. Jesus might be the fulfilment of various expectations among the Jewish people of the time. John the Baptist had made a great impression on the people and had subsequently been killed by Herod Antipas, another son of Herod the Great. Had he been raised from the dead? The book of Malachi had spoken of the return of the prophet Elijah (*Malachi* 4:5-6 or 3:23-24). Could Jesus be a reborn Elijah? There was also the promise of a great prophet like Moses (*Deuteronomy* 18:15-18). Could Jesus be such a prophet? The evangelist makes no mention of the opinion that Jesus might be the Messiah, thus allowing maximum impact for Peter's words in the next verse.

**v.29** Now Jesus questions the disciples and Peter speaks up: 'You are the Messiah!' It is very likely that, given the impression Jesus made, there was talk among the people of Jesus being the expected Messiah. Hope in the coming of an ideal king, known as *messiah* in Hebrew, and in Greek as *christos*, developed over many centuries. Such hope has its roots in the promise of God of steadfast love to king David (2 *Samuel* 7:15). The book of Isaiah presents portrayals of the ideal Messiah in chapters 9 and 11. Psalm 72 speaks of an ideal king whose reign has no end. Peter and the disciples share this belief. But what expectations do they have of the Messiah, and are such views shared by Jesus? The 'Psalms of Solomon', a non-biblical book containing prayers written in the first century BC though attributed to king Solomon, speaks of a Messiah who would fight for freedom from Roman rule.

**v.30** The reply of Jesus is surprising. He commands the disciples not to repeat what they have said. This is no doubt because their idea of the role of the Messiah is not his idea. Jesus will surprise them still further by speaking of his coming suffering and death.

*Psalm 17 of the 'Psalms of Solomon' reads:*

*See, Lord, and raise up for them their king, the son of David, to rule over your servant Israel in the time known to you, O God.*

*Undergird him with the strength to destroy the unrighteous rulers, to purge Jerusalem from gentiles who trample her to destruction; in wisdom and in righteousness to drive out the sinners from the inheritance.*

# Jesus Speaks of his Death

*In this text, as in many others, Jesus speaks of himself as 'Son of Man'.*

*The meaning of the phrase has been hotly debated among scholars. It may simply be a way of referring to himself instead of saying 'I', but Jesus is fond of quoting the words about a visionary figure, 'one like a son of man', who comes into the presence of God and is rewarded by God in the book of Daniel (7:13). The prophet Ezekiel is often addressed by God with the title 'son of man', which seems to emphasise his humanity and vulnerability. For Jesus, the phrase 'Son of Man' seems to be a humble way of referring to himself and his mission, which has connotations of vulnerability but also of trust in God.*

**v.31** Jesus now speaks for the first time about his death. He will make similar solemn statements in 9:30-32 and in 10:32-34. The whole atmosphere of the gospel changes.

'The Son of Man must undergo great suffering.' There is no escape for Jesus. He is convinced that this is what awaits him. Three groups of people will oppose him. The elders are probably lay members of the Jewish governing body called the Sanhedrin. The chief priests are the present and past high priests, and members of the high priestly families. The scribes are experts in the Jewish law. Jesus will be killed, but will 'rise again' on the third day. This last statement is quite disregarded by Peter in his shock that Jesus is to be killed.

**v.32** Peter is horrified. His ideas about the role of the Messiah do not include suffering such a fate. In his first letter to the Corinthians St Paul writes that the Jews look upon the crucifixion of Christ as a 'scandal' (1 *Corinthians* 1:23). He uses the Greek word *skandalon*, meaning an 'obstacle' or an 'impediment' to belief. In similar fashion the very idea that Jesus should be put to death is a serious obstacle for the faith of the disciples.

**v.33** Jesus' final words leave Peter in no doubt as to his meaning. 'Get behind me, Satan!' he says. In trying to dissuade Jesus, Peter presents a temptation that Jesus should abandon the path he knows he must follow. Those words of rebuke to Peter are also spoken by Jesus at the end of Matthew's detailed account of the temptations of Jesus (*Matthew* 4:13). As he dismissed Satan, so now Jesus dismisses Peter's temptation. It will take time for the disciples to understand and accept the challenge of the cross.

# The Challenge of the Cross

**v.34** The words of Jesus are now addressed not only to the disciples but to the crowd. This is a piece of teaching for all Christians, and it involves the cross. The initial call of Jesus to the disciples made no mention of suffering (*Mark* 1:17), but every disciple learns the challenge of the cross.

**v.35** The challenge of discipleship is spelt out again in this verse as Jesus speaks of the willingness to lose one's life. 'Life' translates the Greek word *psyche*, which also means 'soul' or 'very self'. The Christian is called to be willing to lose everything, but this is the way to life.

**vv.36-37** A further teaching of Jesus suggests that a person's 'life', 'soul' or 'very self' is all a person has. The 'world' here is all the world can offer, all of which, it is implied, is transient. Nothing a person can offer is worth what life is worth, and yet life is not something to cling to. This is the fundamental Christian paradox of the cross.

**v.38** The crucial necessity of following Jesus in this way is underlined in this final piece of teaching. If disciples are ashamed of the humiliation of Jesus, then the Son of Man will be ashamed of them 'when he comes in the glory of his Father'. St Paul declares at the beginning of his Letter to the Romans: 'I am not ashamed of the gospel; for it is the power of God for salvation to everyone who has faith, to the Jew first and also to the Greek.' (*Romans* 1:16) The message of the gospel may be challenging, but it is the way to life. The words of Jesus in verse 38 allude to the gathering of Christ's faithful people at the end of time, which is treated with similar imagery when Jesus talks about the end of time in Mark 13:26-27.

*Jesus' invitation to lose one's life may seem rather strange. St Augustine of Hippo explains:*

*This precept by which we are enjoined to lose our life does not mean that a person should kill himself, which would be an unforgivable crime, but it does mean that one should kill that in oneself which is unduly attached to the earthly, which makes one take inordinate pleasure in this present life to the neglect of the life to come.*

*(Letters, 243, To Laetus)*

*In the parallel story in the Gospel of Matthew Jesus commends Peter for his faith and commissions him as 'the rock' (Matthew 16:18). Eusebius of Caesarea, writing in the fourth century, suggests that, if, as is commonly believed, Mark was reporting the teaching of Peter, then these words of Jesus may have been omitted due to Peter's humility.*

*(Demonstratio evangelica III.3)*

*The famous Dominican biblical scholar, Marie-Joseph Lagrange, wrote in his great commentary on Mark, published in 1911:*

*Mark's intention is not to insist on the organisation of the Church, but on the work and mission of Jesus.*

## The Word Lives On

While the account of the healing of the blind man in Bethsaida is not found in the other gospels, the dialogue between Jesus and Peter is reported. In Matthew's gospel Jesus replies to Peter's confession of faith with the commission: 'You are Peter, and on this rock I will build my church.' (*Matthew* 16:18) In the parallel passage in Luke's gospel (*Luke* 9:18-22) the horrified reaction of Peter to Jesus' words about his coming death is omitted. Luke stresses the fidelity of the disciples and their solidarity with Jesus as he makes his way to Jerusalem.

The words of Jesus about his own fate and his teaching about the cross his disciples must bear are central teachings of the gospel.

## In the Lectionary

The Sunday Lectionary provides for the reading of Mark 8:27-35 on the 24th Sunday of Ordinary Time in Year B.

The complete text we have studied is read on Wednesday, Thursday and Friday of the sixth week in Ordinary Time.

# Live the Word of God

**Listen again to the reading: Mark 8:22-38**

**What do you hear now?**

*Suggestions for reflection and prayer*

**How relevant do you find the idea of 'eyes being opened' when considering matters of faith?**

**Reflect on St Augustine's words about 'losing one's life' at the end of the commentary.**

**How do these central teachings of Jesus challenge us today?**

**Jesus allows time for the blind man to see clearly.**

❖ Pray for patience with ourselves, and with others.

**Jesus, God's expected Messiah, will surprise his disciples.**

❖ Pray for openness to God's ways, and that we may set our minds on divine things and not on human things.

**Jesus challenges his disciples to deny self and to take up the cross.**

❖ Pray for the grace of self-denial and courage, and for generosity in sharing what the world offers.

**Mark writes for a persecuted Church, encouraging believers that the way of suffering leads to life.**

❖ Pray for those persecuted throughout the world today, those whose lives are threatened because of their Christian faith, those who have been traumatised by hatred, and those who are fearful.

**Jesus teaches us not to be ashamed of him or of his teaching.**

❖ Pray for steadfastness in following the way of Jesus.

## Reflect

*St Paul records an ancient Christian hymn:*

*Christ Jesus, though he was in the form of God,*
*did not regard equality with God as something to be exploited, but emptied himself,*
*taking the form of a slave,*
*being born in human likeness.*
*And being found in human form, he humbled himself*
*and became obedient to the point of death – even death on a cross.*

*(Philippians 2:6-8)*

# Jesus the Servant

# Hear the Word of God

## Read Mark 10: 32-45

[32] They were on the road, going up to Jerusalem, and Jesus was walking ahead of them; they were amazed, and those who followed were afraid. He took the twelve aside again and began to tell them what was to happen to him, [33] saying, 'See, we are going up to Jerusalem, and the Son of Man will be handed over to the chief priests and the scribes, and they will condemn him to death; then they will hand him over to the Gentiles; [34] they will mock him, and spit upon him, and flog him, and kill him; and after three days he will rise again.'

[35] James and John, the sons of Zebedee, came forward to him and said to him, 'Teacher, we want you to do for us whatever we ask of you.'

[36] And he said to them, 'What is it you want me to do for you?'

[37] And they said to him, 'Grant us to sit, one at your right hand and one at your left, in your glory.'

[38] But Jesus said to them, 'You do not know what you are asking. Are you able to drink the cup that I drink, or be baptized with the baptism that I am baptized with?'

[39] They replied, 'We are able.'

Then Jesus said to them, 'The cup that I drink you will drink; and with the baptism with which I am baptized, you will be baptized; [40] but to sit at my right hand or at my left is not mine to grant, but it is for those for whom it has been prepared.'

[41] When the ten heard this, they began to be angry with James and John.

[42] So Jesus called them and said to them, 'You know that among the Gentiles those whom they recognize as their rulers lord it over them, and their great ones are tyrants over them. [43] But it is not so among you; but whoever wishes to become great among you must be your servant, [44] and whoever wishes to be first among you must be slave of all. [45] For the Son of Man came not to be served but to serve, and to give his life a ransom for many.'

Facing page: The Procession to Calvary about 1502 by Raphael (1483-1520).

# Understand the Word of God

**This session will explore:**

- ❖ the disciples' struggle to accept the way of the cross
- ❖ the cup to be drunk and the baptism to be faced
- ❖ the call to be a servant
- ❖ the life of Jesus given as 'a ransom for many'
- ❖ the message for today.

## Setting in the Gospel

The journey of Jesus and his disciples to Jerusalem began in chapter 8 of the gospel. At that point we heard Peter declare Jesus to be the Christ, the Messiah, after which Jesus spoke for the first time of his coming suffering, death and resurrection. This is followed by the story of the transfiguration of Jesus, in which the disciples mysteriously receive a foretaste of his coming glory in their experience of Jesus on the mountain (*Mark* 9:2-8). Later in the same chapter Jesus spoke again of his coming death (*Mark* 9:30-32).

In our present text, we hear Jesus speak for the third time of his suffering and death. These three speeches of Jesus punctuate the journey to Jerusalem. They have been compared to the tolling of a bell as Jesus approaches the place of his death. As our text ends, Jesus and the disciples reach Jericho and begin the final ascent to Jerusalem (*Mark* 10:46).

In Fra Angelico's Transfiguration, the apostles are overcome with awe while the Dominican saints contemplate the mystery in faith.

## What Kind of Text?

The text begins with the third announcement by Jesus of his coming suffering, death and resurrection. Comparison between the three announcements (8:31-33  9:30-32  10:32-34) shows that this final speech contains far more detail. Some writers have wondered whether what Jesus actually said has been elaborated using details from Mark's story of the death of Jesus in chapters 14-15.

There follows the dialogue between Jesus and the two brothers, which leads into the teaching of Jesus to the whole group of disciples about being a servant.

# Commentary: verse by verse reading

## Jesus Speaks of his Death for the Third Time

**v.32** Mark describes Jesus and the disciples continuing on their way to Jerusalem. Jesus goes ahead of them, courageously leading the way to the place of martyrdom. The text says that 'they were amazed'. Were the disciples amazed at Jesus' commitment to go resolutely to the place of his death? It may be more accurate to translate the Greek word used here (*ethambounto*) as 'they were anxious', which fits the context better. 'Those who followed were afraid.' This seems to refer to another group of followers, who are fearful of going to Jerusalem, because it is the place where popular, straight-talking prophets face danger. Mark is providing a realistic picture of the trepidation among the twelve, and the other followers of Jesus.

*In Acts 4:27 Peter says:*

*For in this city, in fact, both Herod and Pontius Pilate, with the Gentiles and the peoples of Israel, gathered together against your holy servant Jesus.*

*In the light of the terrible history of anti-Judaism, recent Church teaching has very carefully stressed that responsibility for the death of Jesus 'cannot be charged against all the Jews then alive without distinction, nor against the Jews of today.'*

*(Vatican II, Declaration on the Relationship of the Church to Non-Christian Religions, Nostra Aetate, n.4)*

**v.33** The emphasis on 'going up' to Jerusalem reminds us of the city's location on a hill-top, and indicates that the journey is coming to its final stages. Jesus has followed the valley of the river Jordan to this point, and will soon begin the ascent towards Jerusalem.

Once again Jesus speaks of himself as 'the Son of Man', which suggests his readiness to take the road of suffering but also his trust in the protection of the Father. As in Mark 8:32, the chief priests and the scribes are mentioned, but there is no mention here of the elders. What is quite new is the statement that 'they will hand him over to the Gentiles'. This points to the part played in the death of Jesus by the Roman authorities. Christian reflection sought to elucidate the roles played in bringing about the death of Jesus by some Jews and some Gentiles.

**v.34** This verse refers to the treatment of Jesus in some detail, and some of the expressions used here are found again during the story of the passion in Mark 15:19-20. As with the previous two passion announcements, the third also ends with reference to 'rising again'.

# The Request of James and John

**vv.35-36** The disciples James and John, the sons of Zebedee, were called by Jesus in Mark 1:19-20. With Peter they form something of an inner circle of disciples, being allowed to witness the healing of Jairus' daughter (*Mark* 5:37), and being with Jesus on the mountain of the transfiguration (*Mark* 9:2). The two disciples address Jesus as 'teacher'. Though Jesus' words often surprise them, they are still willing to learn, and the nature of their request will reveal the extent of their need to learn.

**v.37** Imagining their future in the kingdom of Jesus, they request seats at the right and left of Jesus. This is an interesting request. In the ancient world being on the right is often understood as being in the place of honour, while being on the left is not. The dramatic scene of the last judgement portrayed by Jesus in Matthew's gospel has the sheep, representing the virtuous, on the right, and the goats, representing the wicked, on the left (*Matthew* 25:33). Despite this, in the present context, a seat on the left is also a place of honour. The two disciples are keen to be present in the 'glory' of Jesus, in other words, to share his triumph.

The First Shall Be the Last, illustration for 'The Life of Christ' by James Jacques Joseph Tissot, (1836-1902)

The chapel of St John in the Oil (San Giovanni in Oleo), commemorates John's suffering.

**v.38** While the disciples' ideas about the role of the Messiah have to be revised to include the prospect of suffering and death, Jesus must also challenge the incomplete ideas about discipleship entertained by James and John. To be a follower of Jesus includes drinking his cup and being baptized with his baptism. The cup is frequently used in the Scriptures as a symbol both of joy and of pain. In the garden of Gethsemane Jesus will pray: 'Abba, Father, for you all things are possible; remove this cup from me; yet, not what I want, but what you want.' (*Mark* 14:36) Drinking the cup becomes a way of referring to Christian martyrdom. The symbol of baptism suggests immersion in suffering.

**v.39** The quick reply of James and John may remind us of Peter's hasty promise of facing death for Jesus (*Mark* 14:31). We learn from the Acts of the Apostles that James did indeed suffer martyrdom at the command of Herod Agrippa, the grandson of Herod the Great (*Acts* 12:2). The traditions about the death of John are more complex. In the work called the 'Acts of John', written probably in the 2nd century and containing apocryphal traditions about John, we are told that John died a natural death at Ephesus. Later traditions claim that he had survived drinking deadly poison, and that he had emerged unscathed from boiling oil.

**v.40** Despite their readiness to suffer martyrdom Jesus does not promise the brothers places of honour. He says: 'It is for those for whom it has been prepared.' Matthew will clarify these words by adding 'prepared by my Father' (*Matthew* 20:23). The Father prepares the final destiny of the disciples, as he does for the Son. St Paul writes that 'no eye has seen, nor ear heard, nor the human heart conceived, what God has prepared for those who love him' (1 *Corinthians* 2:9).

# Jesus Teaches the Disciples

**vv.41-42** The annoyance of the other ten disciples at the ambition of James and John leads Jesus to give some significant teaching, which Mark introduces in solemn fashion: 'Jesus called them and said to them.' Jesus points to the bad example of the rulers of the Gentiles, who 'lord it over them' and 'are tyrants over them'. This is not to be the habit among the disciples of Jesus. In the First Letter of Peter the teaching of Jesus is faithfully passed on, when the writer urges the elders: 'Do not lord it over those in your charge, but be examples to the flock." (1 *Peter* 5:3)

**vv.43-44** When Jesus had previously spoken about his coming death, the disciples had argued about their status. Jesus had said: 'Whoever wants to be first must be last of all and servant of all.' (*Mark* 9:35) This teaching about service is taken further now. The one who wishes to be great must be a servant. The one who wishes to be first must be a slave. While the servant (Greek *diakonos*) might serve at the table in the master's house, the slave (Greek *doulos*) would have more arduous tasks. In the opening verse of the Letter to the Romans Paul refers to himself as 'slave' of Jesus Christ. Paul freely takes the condition of slave: 'For though I am free with respect to all, I have made myself a slave to all.' (1 *Corinthians* 9:19)  The teaching of Jesus in Mark's gospel is lived out by the disciples of Jesus.

**v.45** Once again Jesus refers to himself as 'the Son of Man'. He is to give his life as a 'ransom for many'. The ransom (Greek *lutron*) is the price paid for freedom. The word can refer to the ransom paid to free captives taken in war, and to the price paid when a person's life might be forfeited. Jesus is the ransom for all. He becomes a slave in order to ransom people from slavery. The First Letter to Timothy reads: 'He gave himself a ransom for all.' (1 *Timothy* 2:6), and in the Letter to Titus we read: 'He it is who gave himself for us that he might redeem us from all iniquity.' (*Titus* 2:14)

*That Jesus should take the role of a servant or a slave does not square with the expected notions of being the Messiah. But in the second part of the Book of Isaiah we find the well-known poems about the 'suffering servant' (Isaiah 42:1-4 49:1-6 50:4-9 52:13-53:12). The servant is sent to preach, to bring good news to the nations, to be a light, but the servant must also suffer persecution, and gives his life for others. It seems clear that Jesus was inspired by these texts in his mission of service. It is certainly true that the early Christians saw these poems as preparation for the coming of Jesus and as fulfilled by Jesus. Jesus brings together the roles of Messiah and Servant.*

*Jesus did not wish to be a political Messiah who would dominate by force but preferred to call himself the Son of Man who came to serve, and 'to give his life as a ransom for many' (Mark 10:45). He showed himself as the perfect Servant of God who 'will not break a bruised reed or quench a smouldering wick'*

*(Matthew 12:20).*

*(Vatican II, Declaration on Religious Liberty, Dignitatis Humanae, n.11)*

## The Word Lives On

All three synoptic gospels contain Jesus' third announcement of his coming death, but Luke completely omits the story about James and John, playing down the inadequacies of the disciples, as is his custom.

In Matthew it is their mother who makes the request of Jesus (*Matthew* 20:20). Perhaps this is the evangelist's way of excusing the rather awkward request of the sons of Zebedee. In Matthew's account too there is reference only to the cup they will drink and not to baptism, perhaps because such an apparently negative reference to baptism might create confusion in Christian minds (*Matthew* 20:22).

## In the Lectionary

The Sunday Lectionary provides for the reading of Mark 10:35-45 on the 29th Sunday in Ordinary Time in Year B.

The complete text is read on Wednesday of the eighth week in Ordinary Time.

*Serve one another, and when you do, do it in love for me.*
*('This is my body' v.5 words by Damian Lundy)*

# Live the Word of God

**Listen again to the reading: Mark 10:32-45**

**What do you hear now?**

*Suggestions for reflection and prayer*

**What strikes you most forcefully about this passage?**

**Reflect on the words of St John Chrysostom on this page, particularly the final question.**

**How is the role of 'servant' regarded in today's world?**

**Jesus courageously leads the disciples on the way to Jerusalem.**

❖ Pray that we may overcome the fears which hinder a more generous response to the gospel.

**Disciples still face martyrdom for the gospel.**

❖ Pray for all faith communities whose lives are under threat because of their beliefs.

**The disciples James and John are ambitious for places in glory.**

❖ Pray for the gift of humility and the serenity to accept whatever the Father has prepared for us.

**The disciples are taught not to lord it over others.**

❖ Pray that when we exercise authority we may learn how to lead and inspire without domineering.

**The servant of the Lord gives his life as a ransom for others.**

❖ Pray for the courage to serve and to give our lives for others.

## Reflect

*St John Chrysostom writes:*

*Before he humbled himself, only the angels knew him. After he humbled himself, all human nature knew him. You see how his humbling of himself did not make him have less but produced countless benefits, countless deeds of virtue, and made his glory shine forth with greater brightness. God wants for nothing and has need of nothing. Yet, when he humbled himself, he produced such great good, increased his household, and extended his kingdom. Why, then, are you afraid that you will become less if you humble yourself?*

*(On the Incomprehensible Nature of God 8.47)*

*From the second preface for Easter:*

*He has made us children of the light, rising to new and everlasting life.*
*He has opened the gates of heaven to receive his faithful people*
*His death is our ransom from death; his resurrection is our rising to life.*

# Jesus in the Temple

# Hear the Word of God

## Read Mark 11:12-25

¹² On the following day, when they came from Bethany, he was hungry. ¹³ Seeing in the distance a fig tree in leaf, he went to see whether perhaps he would find anything on it. When he came to it, he found nothing but leaves, for it was not the season for figs. ¹⁴ He said to it, 'May no one ever eat fruit from you again.' And his disciples heard it.

¹⁵ Then they came to Jerusalem. And he entered the temple and began to drive out those who were selling and those who were buying in the temple, and he overturned the tables of the money changers and the seats of those who sold doves; ¹⁶ and he would not allow anyone to carry anything through the temple. ¹⁷ He was teaching and saying, 'Is it not written, 'My house shall be called a house of prayer for all the nations'? But you have made it a den of robbers.'

¹⁸ And when the chief priests and the scribes heard it, they kept looking for a way to kill him; for they were afraid of him, because the whole crowd was spellbound by his teaching. ¹⁹ And when evening came, Jesus and his disciples went out of the city.

²⁰ In the morning as they passed by, they saw the fig tree withered away to its roots. ²¹ Then Peter remembered and said to him, 'Rabbi, look! The fig tree that you cursed has withered.'

²² Jesus answered them, 'Have faith in God. ²³ Truly I tell you, if you say to this mountain, 'Be taken up and thrown into the sea', and if you do not doubt in your heart, but believe that what you say will come to pass, it will be done for you. ²⁴ So I tell you, whatever you ask for in prayer, believe that you have received it, and it will be yours. ²⁵ Whenever you stand praying, forgive, if you have anything against anyone; so that your Father in heaven may also forgive you your trespasses.'

Facing page: Purification of the Temple by the Spanish artist El Greco.
He painted this scene several times. This version is thought to have been completed in 1600.

# Understand the Word of God

**This session will explore:**

- ❖ Jesus' arrival in Jerusalem
- ❖ the significance of the cursing of the fig tree
- ❖ the cleansing of the temple
- ❖ Jesus' teaching about prayer and forgiveness
- ❖ the message for today.

## Setting in the Gospel

In this gospel passage we find Jesus at his destination, the city of Jerusalem. Remember how the evangelist Mark has put his gospel together. He began with the material about the preaching of the kingdom and the miracles Jesus worked in the north, in his home region of Galilee. The journey of Jesus and his disciples to Jerusalem began in chapter 8 of the gospel. That journey was marked by a growing sense of foreboding as Jesus repeatedly attempted to prepare the disciples for his approaching death.

Detail from a fresco depicting Christ's entry into Jerusalem from the Story of the Passion of Christ by Pietro Lorenzetti c.1321.

At the beginning of chapter 11 Jesus enters Jerusalem. He enters the city a few days before the feast of Passover, when Jerusalem was filling up with pilgrims coming to celebrate the feast. Jesus rides a donkey, entering the city in humility. The significance of this action is explained in Matthew's gospel, for Matthew quotes the words of the prophet Zechariah about the coming of a humble Messiah (*Matthew* 21:4-5). The entry into Jerusalem on the donkey is the first of several significant actions of Jesus. We are exploring in particular detail the accounts of the cursing of the fig-tree and the cleansing of the temple, which follow directly after Jesus' triumphal entry.

# What Kind of Text?

The first section of our text, vv.12-14, concerns the cursing of the fig-tree. This is a curious and difficult story. It is often included among the miracles of Jesus, for Jesus displays extraordinary power, but, whereas Jesus usually employs his power to heal, the power of Jesus in this instance is used to inflict harm on the tree.

What kind of text are we dealing with here? It is useful to note that among the prophets of Israel the fig-tree is sometimes the symbol of the people. In the book of the prophet Jeremiah we read: 'There are no grapes on the vine, nor figs on the fig tree.' (*Jeremiah* 8:13). The prophet's words suggest that the people are unresponsive to God's call, bearing no fruit. The cursing of the fig-tree by Jesus is intended to point to the lack of response of the people of his day. Jesus' action is symbolic, illustrating this lack of response.

The prophets of Israel often perform symbolic actions in order to bring their message alive. We read in Jeremiah 19 how the prophet is told to take an earthenware jug and break it in full sight of the people. This destructive action was a symbol of what was in store for the people of Israel. In Ezekiel 37 we read that the prophet brings two sticks together in order to proclaim the reunification of Israel and Judah. When the prophets performed such symbolic actions, the people asked what they meant, and were led to reflection and new understanding. Similarly, Jesus' symbolic actions make people think.

The following section, vv.15-19, is the narrative often known as the 'cleansing of the temple'. This is a further symbolic action, which raises questions about the anger and violence of Jesus.

Our text concludes with the discovery of the withered fig-tree, and Jesus' teaching about prayer and forgiveness in vv.20-25.

## Commentary: verse by verse reading
## The Cursing of the Fig-tree

**v.12** In Mark's account this is now the second day of the presence of Jesus in Jerusalem. The previous evening Jesus had briefly visited the temple for the first time before going to nearby Bethany to spend the night (*Mark* 11:11). Bethany lies about two miles to the east of Jerusalem, on the slopes of the Mount of Olives. The Gospel of John tells us that Martha, Mary and Lazarus lived at Bethany (*John* 11:1), and Mark will tell us of the anointing of the head of Jesus in the house of Simon the leper at Bethany (*Mark* 14:3). Perhaps Bethany was a safer location than Jerusalem for Jesus to spend the night.

*St Augustine comments on the withered fig-tree as follows:*

*What terrible things had the poor tree done simply in not bearing fruit? Could the tree reasonably be faulted for its fruitlessness? No. But human beings who by their own free will decide not to bear fruit – that is a different matter. Those found wanting in accountability in this case are those who had the benefit of the law, which was meant to bear fruit, but they had no fruit to show for it. They had a full growth of leaves (the law), yet they bore no fruit (works of mercy).*

*(Sermons on New Testament Lessons 48.3)*

**v.13** Mark makes it quite clear that the fig-tree is in leaf, but that it was not yet the season for figs. To look for figs in March or April, in the days approaching the feast of Passover, is quite unreasonable, but the action of Jesus here is symbolic. Jesus the prophet is using the fig-tree to symbolise the lack of fruitfulness among the people of Israel. The theme of fruitfulness returns in the parable of the tenants in chapter 12, where the tenants are unwilling to yield the fruit for the land-owner. The message of Jesus in both texts is plain: it is a judgement on those who do not produce fruit and a challenge to produce fruit in the service of God.

**v.14** Mark tells us that the disciples heard the curse. In this way he prepares us for the continuation of the story in verse 20, after Jesus has visited the temple.

# The Cleansing of the Temple

**v.15** The disturbance created by Jesus in the temple is another example of a symbolic action. How else can we explain such behaviour? To provide for the needs of temple sacrifice, animals and birds, but also wine, oil, and salt, would have been sold in the outer court, known as the Court of the Gentiles. Leviticus chapter 2 tells how wine, oil and salt were added to some offerings. Cattle and sheep, and also doves, would be used for sacrifices, the doves being a sacrifice the poor could afford (*Leviticus* 12:8). At the same time, it was necessary for pilgrims to pay the temple tax, as laid down in Exodus 30:13. This tax had to be paid in Jewish coinage. Greek and Roman coins were not accepted, so money had to be changed, and the money-changers made their profit. No doubt those who bought material for temple sacrifice were also charged heavy rates. All this activity turns the outer court of the temple into a marketplace.

**v.16** Jewish law prohibited using the temple as a short-cut. The traditional collection of law known as the Mishnah, compiled at the end of the second century AD, reads as follows: 'A man may not enter into the Temple Mount with his staff or his sandal or his wallet, or with the dust upon his feet, nor may he make of it a short-cut; still less may he spit there.' (*Tractate Berakoth* 9.5)

**v.17** Jesus uses texts of Scripture to explain his action. The quotation, from Isaiah 56:7, reads 'My house shall be called a house of prayer for all the nations.' The commercialisation of the temple means that foreigners, who are allowed to worship in the Court of the Gentiles, have seen their area of prayer turned into a marketplace. Jesus' anger is against those who do not respect the right of foreigners to worship in the temple. The phrase 'den of robbers' is taken from Jeremiah 7:11. Jesus' anger here is against those who exploit worshippers by charging exorbitant prices and enforcing extortionate rates for changing money. The anger of Jesus is not directed at temple worship, or at the system of temple sacrifices. It is the anger of a prophet who challenges the injustice inflicted on vulnerable people.

*In Luke's gospel we read of the offering made by Mary and Joseph at the presentation of Jesus, 'a pair of turtle-doves or two young pigeons' (Luke 2:22-24). In Matthew's gospel we read the strange story of the coming of the collectors of the temple tax to Peter. Jesus gives instructions to Peter, that he will find a coin in a fish's mouth, but we never hear how the story ends (Matthew 17:24-27).*

*Why is this action of Jesus referred to as the 'cleansing of the temple'? Reference to further Old Testament texts provides the answer. In Malachi 3:1-3 the prophet speaks of the coming of God's messenger who will purify the temple, and in Zechariah 14:21 it is foreseen that when the day of the Lord comes there will be no more traders in the temple. As well as being a prophetic act of judgement, Jesus' cleansing of the temple is also a messianic act. The symbolic action proclaims judgement on injustice, but also the coming of the one expected by the prophets.*

**v.18** It is understandable that the priests, who control the temple, and the scribes, who teach there, are incensed by Jesus' behaviour. There is another reference to plots to kill Jesus. We first heard of such plots in Mark 3:6. On this occasion, however, Jesus is in Jerusalem, where the religious authorities have great influence and there is a strong Roman military presence at the time of the feast. The danger for Jesus is clearly greater in Jerusalem. Mark nevertheless makes clear that the ordinary people are attracted to the teaching of Jesus. In this case Mark seems to be pointing to their approval of his extraordinary actions in the temple. While the ordinary folk have admired the teaching of Jesus from the very start of his ministry, the priests and scribes are afraid of him.

**v.19** At the end of the day Jesus and his disciples once again return to the comparative safety of Bethany.

Below: Model of Jerusalem at the time of the Second Temple. The Temple dominates the skyline.

# Jesus Teaches the Disciples

**v.20** On the following morning it is discovered that the fig-tree has withered. This is the trigger for some teaching of Jesus about prayer.

**vv.21-22** Peter's reaction to this sign of Jesus' power seems enthusiastic. This is perhaps why Jesus changes the subject. Instead of teaching about Israel's need to produce fruit, Jesus begins to talk about faith.

**v.23** Jesus introduces this teaching by using the expression 'Amen', translated here as 'Truly'. The power of unhesitating prayer is illustrated by reference to moving mountains. Matthew uses the example twice in his gospel, once in this context (*Matthew* 21:21), and on another occasion when the disciples had insufficient faith to heal the epileptic boy (*Matthew* 17:20). St Paul writes in the First Letter to the Corinthians: 'If I have all faith, so as to remove mountains, but do not have love, I am nothing.' (1 *Corinthians* 13:2).

**v.24** Jesus repeats his teaching on having faith while at prayer in unambiguous terms.

**v.25** This verse takes the teaching on prayer further to include the need for forgiveness. It may well be that the evangelist has gathered together various teachings of Jesus about prayer at this point as part of his editorial activity. We cannot be sure Jesus taught these things at this precise time and in this place. There are some similarities here with the words of Jesus in the Sermon on the Mount. Jesus talks there too about 'standing to pray' (*Matthew* 6:5), and about asking 'the Father in heaven' (*Matthew* 6:9) for forgiveness *(Matthew* 6:14)

*'Amen'*

*The word 'Amen' is originally from the Aramaic language, the native language of Jesus. It means 'truly' or 'indeed', and emphasises the reliability of what is being said. It is found on the lips of Jesus in all four gospels. Mark also includes other Aramaic expressions, transcribed into Greek letters so that the Aramaic words can be read in a Greek text. In Mark 5:41 we read 'Talitha cum', 'Little girl, get up!' Jesus says to the deaf and dumb man in Mark 9:34 'Ephphatha', which means 'Be opened'. In the garden of Gethsemane Jesus begins his prayer by calling out 'Abba', which is Aramaic for 'Father' (Mark 14:36).*

## The Word Lives On

Matthew makes the cursing of the fig-tree more dramatic by stating that the fig-tree withered at once (*Matthew* 21:19), inferring that the powerful word of Jesus must have had immediate effect. In his account of the cleansing of the temple, which, unlike in Mark, happens at Jesus' very first entry into Jerusalem, there is a curious detail. Matthew tells us that 'the blind and the lame came to him in the temple, and he cured them' (*Matthew* 21:14). The blind and the lame may well have been confined to the outer court due to their disabilities. Matthew seems to be saying that Jesus, as master of the temple, challenges the rules of the temple and opens it up to all.

In his gospel Luke diminishes the violence of Jesus, giving the briefest possible description of the cleansing of the temple (*Luke* 19:45). Luke also omits the story of the cursing of the tree. It has sometimes been suggested that Luke's parable of the fruitless fig-tree in the vineyard in Luke 13:6-9 has taken the place of this narrative.

In John's gospel the story of the cleansing of the temple is found at the very start of the ministry of Jesus in John 2:13-17. The difference of location of the incident in the different gospels reminds us that the evangelists ordered their material sometimes for historical reasons and sometimes for reasons of emphasis. For John, when Jesus enters the city of Jerusalem for the first time, he must enter the temple, and, when he enters the temple, he purifies it as is expected of the Messiah.

## In the Lectionary

Mark 11:11-26 is found in the weekday lectionary and is read on the Friday of the eighth week of Ordinary Time.

# Live the Word of God

**Listen again to the reading: Mark 11:12-25**

**What do you hear now?**

*Suggestions for reflection and prayer*

**What in particular strikes you about Jesus' actions in this passage?**

**Reflect on the words of St Augustine at the beginning of the commentary.**

**How can we ensure that the Church is 'a house of prayer for all the nations'?**

A call to prayer?

The Angel of the North dominates the skyline for motorists on the A1.

**Jesus curses the fig-tree as a sign to the people.**

❖ Pray that we may bear fruit for Christ by performing what St Augustine calls the 'works of mercy'.

**Jesus expresses his anger at the exploitation of worshippers.**

❖ Pray for the courage to speak out against injustice, aware that we too are in constant need of conversion.

**Jesus teaches us to protect and foster the holiness of God's house.**

❖ Pray for the sensitivity to respect our churches as places of worship and welcome, silence and prayer.

**Reflect**

*St John Chysostom writes on prayer:*

*Prayer is a mighty weapon, a treasure undiminished, a mine never exhausted, a sky unobstructed by clouds, a haven unruffled by storm. It is the root, the fountain, and the mother of a thousand blessings.*

*(On the Incomprehensibility of God, 5.44)*

**Jesus teaches respect for the rights of all.**

❖ Pray for the generosity to receive with respect and affection all who enter God's house, and to reach out to those who are lost.

**Jesus teaches us to pray without doubting and with a forgiving heart.**

❖ Ask for the gift of prayer, for trust in the goodness of God, for the ability to forgive as we pray to be forgiven, and for fidelity to prayer with the local church.

# The Coming of the Son of Man

# Hear the Word of God

## Read Mark 13:14-32

[14] Jesus said, 'But when you see the desolating sacrilege set up where it ought not to be (let the reader understand), then those in Judea must flee to the mountains; [15] the one on the housetop must not go down or enter the house to take anything away; [16] the one in the field must not turn back to get a coat. [17] Woe to those who are pregnant and to those who are nursing infants in those days! [18] Pray that it may not be in winter. [19] For in those days there will be suffering, such as has not been from the beginning of the creation that God created until now, no, and never will be. [20] And if the Lord had not cut short those days, no one would be saved; but for the sake of the elect, whom he chose, he has cut short those days.

[21] And if anyone says to you at that time, 'Look! Here is the Messiah!' or 'Look! There he is!' - do not believe it. [22] False messiahs and false prophets will appear and produce signs and omens, to lead astray, if possible, the elect. [23] But be alert; I have already told you everything.

[24] But in those days, after that suffering, the sun will be darkened, and the moon will not give its light, [25] and the stars will be falling from heaven, and the powers in the heavens will be shaken. [26] Then they will see 'the Son of Man coming in clouds' with great power and glory. [27] Then he will send out the angels, and gather his elect from the four winds, from the ends of the earth to the ends of heaven.

[28] From the fig tree learn its lesson: as soon as its branch becomes tender and puts forth its leaves, you know that summer is near. [29] So also, when you see these things taking place, you know that he is near, at the very gates. [30] Truly I tell you, this generation will not pass away until all these things have taken place. [31] Heaven and earth will pass away, but my words will not pass away. [32] But about that day or hour no one knows, neither the angels in heaven, nor the Son, but only the Father.'

Facing page: The Son of God - The Word of God, by Victor Mikhailovich Vasnetsov, (1848-1926)

# Understand the Word of God

**This session will explore:**

- ❖ Jesus' final teaching in Jerusalem
- ❖ the abomination of desolation
- ❖ the gathering of Christ's people at the end of time
- ❖ Jesus' teaching about the end
- ❖ the message for today.

## Setting in the Gospel

In Mark's account of the ministry, Jesus entered Jerusalem for the first time in chapter 11, causing confusion on the next day as he performed his symbolic action of cleansing the temple. Mark reports further extensive teaching of Jesus throughout chapters 11 and 12. He reaches profound agreement with one of the scribes when questioned about the greatest commandment of the law (*Mark* 12:28-34). He criticises the ostentatious behaviour of the scribes who parade about in their long robes (*Mark* 12:38-40). He upholds the example of the poor widow who contributes all she has to the temple treasury (*Mark* 12:41-44).

When we reach chapter 13 we find a new collection of teaching of Jesus. The whole chapter considers questions about the future, in particular the fate of Jerusalem and the end of time. Jesus gives this teaching on the Mount of Olives, looking over the Kidron Valley to the temple which lies opposite. Jesus speaks about the troubles that his followers will have to endure, including wars, natural disasters and persecutions. The chapter comes to something of a climax with Jesus' words about the 'desolating sacrilege', often referred to as the 'abomination of desolation', which seems to refer to a future desecration of the temple in Jerusalem (vv.14-23). We will also consider Jesus' words about the return of the Son of Man and the gathering together of his people (vv.24-27). Finally, we will examine further teaching of Jesus about the time of the end (vv.28-32).

## What Kind of Text?

The material in this chapter, about the future and the end of time, is of a very specific type and is similar in theme to what we read in the Old Testament book of Daniel. In chapters 7-12 of that book we find Daniel's strange visions concerning the future, the destruction of those who persecute God's people, and the reward given to God's holy ones.

These visions contain images of strange animals, with horns representing strength. Jesus does not employ this kind of imagery, but the subject matter of Mark 13 is similar to that of the visions of Daniel: it concerns the future triumph of God's people. Daniel's visions are known as 'apocalyptic', which means that they 'reveal' secrets about the future. For this reason this chapter is sometimes referred to as the 'apocalypse' of Mark.

*Apocalyptic writing became popular in the 2nd century BC during times of persecution. There are many instances of such writing in Judaism, most of which did not find their way into the Scriptures. In the New Testament the Book of Revelation is another example of such writing. The visionary, whose name is John, witnesses the triumph of God and the Lamb, who represents Christ, over the power of the Roman empire. Christian apocalypses naturally give a prominent role to Christ as the one through whom the victory of God is won. Images from the book of Daniel and from other parts of the Jewish Scriptures abound in the Book of Revelation.*

Sir Jacob Epstein's Christ in Majesty, Llandaff Cathedral.

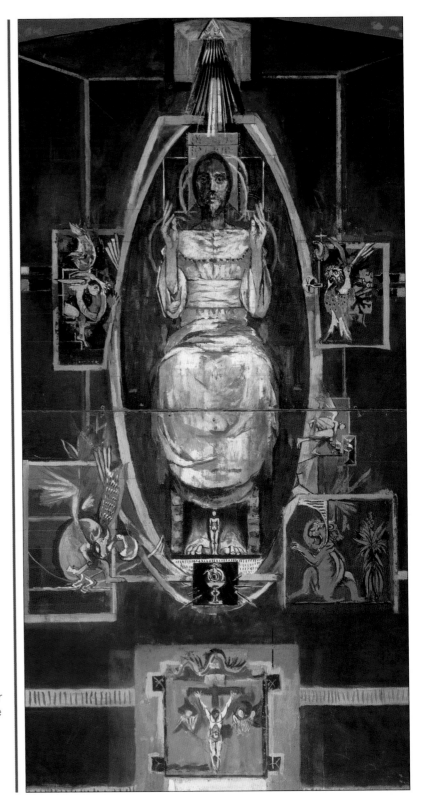

Graham Sutherland's final cartoon for his striking tapestry in Coventry Cathedral. On either side of the seated Christ are the traditional symbolic figures for the four evangelists and at his feet a human figure wrapped in grave clothes.

# Commentary: verse by verse reading

## The Desolating Sacrilege

**v.14** The 'desolating sacrilege' is a curious and difficult expression. It is referred to more commonly as the 'abomination of desolation'. Not surprisingly, given what we have already discovered about the passage, this phrase originates in the book of Daniel. In his visions Daniel is told about the 'desolating sacrilege', or the 'desolating abomination'. The phrase seems to refer to the desecration of the temple of God in Jerusalem which took place when the pagan king Antiochus Epiphanes set up a pagan altar there. Daniel 9:27 says this about the king: 'He shall make sacrifice and offering cease, and in their place shall be an abomination that desolates, until the decreed end is poured out upon the desolator.' This strange language referring to the desecration of the holiness of the temple by Antiochus is used by Jesus to speak of the coming desecration of the temple by the Roman occupiers.

**vv.15-16** Jesus describes situations in which people can be caught unprepared, and encourages immediate flight once people see the sign of the desolating sacrilege.

**v.17** Those who are pregnant or nursing their children are singled out as particularly vulnerable.

**v.18** Winter weather in Palestine would bring flooded wadis, muddy roads, and could even include snow and ice.

**v.19** In this verse Mark speaks of the coming suffering using the Greek word *thlipsis*, which might also be translated as 'tribulation' or 'distress'. The idea of a great tribulation is also taken from the apocalyptic visions of Daniel. In Daniel 12:1 it precedes the resurrection of the virtuous.

**v.20** 'For the sake of the elect' the days of suffering are reduced. This prepares us for the gathering of the elect in v.27. The chapter repeatedly affirms that the people of Christ have nothing to fear since God has control over the events of the end-time.

**vv.21-23** These verses return to the theme of false Messiahs and false prophets which was treated earlier in vv.5-6.

*Antiochus Epiphanes IV belonged to the Seleucid dynasty which took over power in Syria on the break-up of the empire of Alexander the Great. Antiochus Epiphanes controlled Palestine from 175 to 164 BC, and was notorious for his persecution of the Jewish faith. The two books of Maccabees narrate his persecution and the subsequent fight for freedom of the Jewish people under the leadership of Judas Maccabeus and his brothers. The first two chapters of the first book of Maccabees provide a good idea about the persecution instigated by Antiochus and the Jewish response to it. The traumatic events of the 2nd century BC fired the faith and imagination of the Jewish people so that any pagan invasion or oppression was seen as a challenge to God's rule. Jesus naturally uses the language which arose from this crisis to speak of future hope despite the Roman oppression of the time.*

# The Coming of the Son of Man

*The Christian hymn for funerals known as the 'Dies irae' is based on material from Zephaniah. It stresses the awfulness of the day of judgement. Christians need to remember too that the day of judgement is for the virtuous the day of salvation and of being gathered together into Christ's kingdom.*

*St Bede teaches:*

*The stars at the day of judgment will seem to be dark, not by any failure of their own lustre, but in consequence of the increase of the true light throwing them into the shade.*

*(Homilies on the Gospels)*

*The period between the first and second coming of the Lord is the time of missionary activity, when, like the harvest, the Church will be gathered from the four winds into the kingdom of God. For the gospel must be preached to all the nations before the Lord comes.*

*(Vatican II, Decree on the Missionary Activity of the Church n.9)*

**vv.24-25** The final events take on a massive scale. In these verses Jesus uses language which is common in the prophets when they speak about 'the day of the Lord', the day of judgement. In the book of Isaiah we read: 'The stars of the heavens and their constellations will not give their light; the sun will be dark at its rising, and the moon will not shed its light.' (*Isaiah* 13:10). A later prophet called Zephaniah describes the day of judgement as 'a day of darkness and gloom' (*Zephaniah* 1:15). It is important to remember that Jesus is using customary expressions to speak about something which lies beyond human understanding. Such apocalyptic language need not be taken literally, but evokes the mighty power of God as the day of Christ's return arrives.

**v.26** The return of Jesus at the end of time is described as the coming of 'the Son of Man in clouds with great power and glory'. To understand this statement better we need once again to refer to the book of Daniel. In the most important of his visions, Daniel sees 'one like a son of man', coming on the clouds of heaven (*Daniel* 7:13). This figure, who represents those who have been martyred during the persecution of Antiochus, comes into the presence of God to receive power and glory. The interpretation of this vision is that the martyrs receive the reward of life with God. Jesus, who has already spoken on several occasions of his own death and resurrection, uses the text of Daniel to speak of his return in glory. Jesus will use this verse of the book of Daniel again when he stands before the high-priest and says: 'You will see the Son of Man seated at the right hand of the Power and coming with the clouds of heaven.' (*Mark* 14:62). On both occasions Jesus is using Scripture to speak of his own future triumph.

**v.27** Jesus speaks of the gathering together of the 'elect', those who are chosen. This should be understood as those from all corners of the earth who have committed themselves to following Christ. Matthew's gospel gives a fuller account of the last judgement in chapter 25, where we hear of the gathering of all the nations before the Son of Man in his glory. Those before him are separated into the 'sheep at his right hand' and the 'goats at his left'. The text of Mark's apocalypse by contrast does not refer to the fate of those who are not among the elect.

Christ in Majesty after Titian's 'Gloria' by Cornelius Cort 1487-1576.
All the human figures are focused on Christ returned to the glory of his father.

# More Sayings about the End

**vv.28-29** Jesus uses the fig-tree as a type of parable. Its breaking into leaf is a sign of the arrival of summer. Similarly, the events Jesus has foretold so far in this chapter point to his imminent return. 'He is near, at the very gates.' The Letter of James uses the same idea when it says: 'The Judge is standing at the doors!' (*James* 5:9). There is a rather different use of the image in one of the letters in the Book of Revelation, when Jesus says to the people of the church in Laodicea: 'Listen! I am standing at the door, knocking.' (*Revelation* 3:20) Christ is at our door throughout our lives seeking to enter.

**v.30** This saying of Jesus begins with the solemn 'Truly, I tell you,' which translates the Aramaic expression 'Amen', and emphasises the importance of what is about to be said. We have already come across the expression in Mark 11:23, where it introduced Jesus' teaching about the power of prayer made with faith. The saying introduced here is not without difficulty. It suggests the imminent fulfilment of all that Jesus has announced. What does Jesus mean by 'this generation'? Does he mean all this should take place within forty years? Is it possible that Jesus was mistaken? Could Jesus be mistaken about such an important issue? Some commentators have suggested that this statement was added by an over-confident editor of the gospel in order to answer people's questions about the time of the end.

**v.31** This verse stresses the reliability of the words of Jesus. In the Sermon on the Mount Jesus says that heaven and earth must first pass away before the law loses its validity (*Matthew* 5:18). A similar statement is made here in relation to the words of Jesus.

**v.32** This final difficult verse seems to be in conflict with the confident statement in verse 30. Jesus says that only the Father, and not even the Son, knows the day and hour of the end. We are faced here with the deep mystery of Jesus' human knowledge of what the Father knows. Jesus, the Son of God, is surely aware of these secrets, for he comes to make God the Father known, but not all the truths of God are to be communicated to us. When, at the beginning of the Acts of the Apostles, the apostles ask Jesus about the time for the restoration

*The Catechism has this to say about the human knowledge of Jesus:*

*By its union to the divine wisdom in the person of the Word incarnate, Christ enjoyed in his human knowledge the fullness of understanding of the eternal plans he had come to reveal. What he admitted to not knowing in this area, he elsewhere declared himself not sent to reveal.*

*(Catechism of Catholic Church 474)*

of Israel, Jesus says: 'It is not for you to know the times or periods that the Father has set by his own authority.' (*Acts* 1:7) This verse of Mark also points to hidden things that we are not allowed to know. The verse also invites us to reflect on the humanity of Jesus and to consider its consequences. The humanity of the Son of God does not lessen his divinity. It reveals to us the humility of God.

Listen! I am standing at the door, knocking.
Christ, the Light of the World,
William Holman Hunt.

## The Word Lives On

Each of the synoptic gospels contains apocalyptic teaching of Jesus similar to that of Mark. Both Mark and Matthew speak of the 'desolating sacrilege', but Matthew provides additional help to the reader by saying that it will be set up in the holy place and that it was 'spoken of by the prophet Daniel' (*Matthew* 24:15). Luke's gospel explains that the desolation will be imminent when Jerusalem is 'surrounded by armies' (*Luke* 21:20). This seems to give a new interpretation to Mark's 'desolating sacrilege' by connecting it to the siege of Jerusalem. He also refers to Jerusalem being 'trampled on by Gentiles' (*Luke* 21:24). When the Son of Man comes Luke gives the following advice: 'When these things begin to take place, stand up and raise your heads, because your redemption is drawing near.' (*Luke* 21:28)

## In the Lectionary

Sayings of Jesus about the future and the end are customarily read towards the end of the liturgical year.

Mark 13:24-32 is read in Year B, on the 33rd Sunday of Ordinary Time, the penultimate Sunday of the liturgical year.

Although the second coming of Christ is a major theme of the first half of the season of Advent, only the final verses of Mark 13 appear in the Advent readings (1st Sunday of Advent Year B).

Human figures are dwarfed by the devastation of an earthquake.

# Live the Word of God

**Listen again to the reading: Mark 13: 14-32**

**What do you hear now?**
*Suggestions for reflection and prayer*

**What do you think was Jesus' intention in speaking to the disciples about the end of time?**

**Reflect on the words of Jesus in Luke 21:28, which are quoted on the previous page.**

**How can Christians be people of hope in a troubled world?**

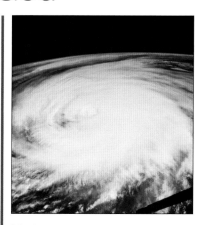

Modern technology provides a dramatic image of a hurricane over the Caribbean.

**Jesus teaches us to be ready for calamities, disasters, and persecutions.**

❖ Pray that we may trust in the presence of Christ whatever sufferings may face us.

**Jesus sends us to bring the good news to the ends of the earth.**

❖ Pray that as members of the Church we may lead men and women to discover the light of the gospel and of the Christian life.

**Jesus will come to gather his elect into his kingdom.**

❖ Pray for a sense of solidarity with all God's people and that we may keep firm our hope in the return of Christ.

**Jesus tells us not to speculate about times and dates.**

❖ Pray for a spirit of preparedness and the grace to live every day in the presence of Christ until he comes in glory.

**Jesus teaches us to live in trust.**

❖ Pray for those who have lost their ability to trust others, and who struggle to believe in a loving God.

**Reflect**

*We read in the Letter to Titus:*

*In the present age let us live lives that are self-controlled, upright, and godly, while we wait for the blessed hope and the manifestation of the glory of our great God and Saviour, Jesus Christ.*

*(Titus 2:12-13)*

# The Last Supper

# Hear the Word of God

## Read Mark 14:12-31

<sup>12</sup> On the first day of Unleavened Bread, when the Passover lamb is sacrificed, his disciples said to him, 'Where do you want us to go and make the preparations for you to eat the Passover?'

<sup>13</sup> So he sent two of his disciples, saying to them, 'Go into the city, and a man carrying a jar of water will meet you; follow him, <sup>14</sup> and wherever he enters, say to the owner of the house, 'The Teacher asks, Where is my guest room where I may eat the Passover with my disciples?' <sup>15</sup> He will show you a large room upstairs, furnished and ready. Make preparations for us there.' <sup>16</sup> So the disciples set out and went to the city, and found everything as he had told them; and they prepared the Passover meal.

<sup>17</sup> When it was evening, he came with the twelve. <sup>18</sup> And when they had taken their places and were eating, Jesus said, 'Truly I tell you, one of you will betray me, one who is eating with me.'

<sup>19</sup> They began to be distressed and to say to him one after another, 'Surely, not I?'

<sup>20</sup> He said to them, 'It is one of the twelve, one who is dipping bread into the bowl with me. <sup>21</sup> For the Son of Man goes as it is written of him, but woe to that one by whom the Son of Man is betrayed! It would have been better for that one not to have been born.'

<sup>22</sup> While they were eating, he took a loaf of bread, and after blessing it he broke it, gave it to them, and said, 'Take: this is my body.'

<sup>23</sup> Then he took a cup, and after giving thanks he gave it to them, and all of them drank from it. <sup>24</sup> He said to them, 'This is my blood of the covenant, which is poured out for many. <sup>25</sup> Truly I tell you, I will never again drink of the fruit of the vine until that day when I drink it new in the kingdom of God.'

<sup>26</sup> When they had sung the hymn, they went out to the Mount of Olives. <sup>27</sup> And Jesus said to them, 'You will all become deserters; for it is written, 'I will strike the shepherd, and the sheep will be scattered.' <sup>28</sup> But after I am raised up, I will go before you to Galilee.'

<sup>29</sup> Peter said to him, 'Even though all become deserters, I will not.'

<sup>30</sup> Jesus said to him, 'Truly I tell you, this day, this very night, before the cock crows twice, you will deny me three times.'

<sup>31</sup> But he said vehemently, 'Even though I must die with you, I will not deny you.' And all of them said the same.

Facing page: The Mafu people are a North Cameroon ethnic group. This is one of a series of New Testament images in their distinctive style.

# Understand the Word of God

**This session will explore:**

❖ the celebration of the Passover

❖ the betrayal by Judas

❖ the origin of the Eucharist

❖ the abandonment by the disciples

❖ the message for today.

## Setting in the Gospel

Mark's account of the public ministry of Jesus ended in chapter 13 with the teaching of Jesus about the future and the end of time. In chapters 14 and 15 we come to what is often called the Passion Narrative, the detailed account of the arrest, trial and crucifixion of Jesus. The fundamental points of Christian preaching from the earliest times were the death and the resurrection of Jesus. If we examine the letters of St Paul, the oldest written documents of the New Testament, and the speeches of the apostles in the Acts of the Apostles, we rapidly become aware that these are the most important statements of Christian faith.

In Mark 11:18 we read how the chief priests and the scribes, on the arrival of Jesus in Jerusalem, plotted how to kill Jesus. Mark 14 begins by taking up this theme again, but the priests and scribes are fearful of the people's reaction: 'Not during the festival, or there may be a riot among the people.' (14:2) After the anointing of the head of Jesus in the house of Simon the leper in Bethany, we hear of the initiative of Judas, who of his own accord approaches the chief priests about betraying Jesus (14:10-11). Our text begins at this point.

*When Peter visits the house of the Roman centurion Cornelius in Caesarea, he says:*

*We are witnesses to all that Jesus of Nazareth did both in Judea and in Jerusalem. They put him to death by hanging him on a tree; but God raised him on the third day.*

*(Acts 10:39-41)*

# What Kind of Text?

The accounts of the events leading up to the death of Jesus are of profound importance for Christians. All four evangelists provide their accounts and they have two major concerns. They seek to provide a historical account of the events leading to the death of Jesus. But they also attempt to explain his death as fulfilment of God's plan. As with all the material in the gospels, so too in the Passion Narrative, there is both an historical and a catechetical intention. The need to explain how the Messiah came to be crucified is in fact the over-riding theological concern. St Paul was well aware of the difficulty raised by the crucifixion of God's Messiah. In the First Letter to the Corinthians he writes: 'We proclaim Christ crucified, a stumbling-block to Jews and foolishness to Gentiles.' (1 *Corinthians* 1:23)

The text we are reading begins with the preparation for the Passover meal by the disciples (vv.12-16). Once Jesus and the twelve gather for the meal Jesus speaks about his betrayal (vv.17-21). The climax of the meal is the institution of the Eucharist (vv.22-25). Finally, as they approach the Mount of Olives, Jesus speaks about his abandonment by the disciples (vv.26-31). Our text is therefore one of great solemnity and sadness.

The Last Supper and the Agony in the Garden, c. 1300 by the Italian School.

## Commentary: verse by verse reading

## Preparations for the Passover

*There is a discrepancy between the synoptic gospels and the Gospel of John concerning the Last Supper. Mark implies that Jesus celebrated the passover meal with his disciples on the night before he died. For John, on the other hand, the passover was going to be celebrated on the following evening, after Jesus had died. This is made clear when the Jews in dialogue with Pilate on the morning after the arrest of Jesus avoid entering Pilate's palace since the defilement they would incur would make them unfit to eat the Passover that evening (John 18:28). Was the last meal of Jesus with his disciples then an anticipation of the Passover? We also must be aware that Jesus does not follow the traditional passover ritual, still celebrated by Jews today.*

**v.12** This verse informs us that Jesus came to Jerusalem at Passover time. The approach of the Passover feast meant that crowds of people would be coming to Jerusalem, some staying in the city and others, like Jesus, finding lodging in nearby villages such as Bethany. The Passover meal was celebrated on the evening of the 14th day of the Jewish month of Nisan. The evening of the day marked the beginning of the feast, which fell on 15th Nisan. This day was also the first of the seven days of Unleavened Bread. Both the feast of Passover and the days of Unleavened Bread commemorate the exodus from Egypt. Passover recalls the story of the angel of the Lord passing over the houses of the Israelites when the plague of the death of the first-born was inflicted (*Exodus* 12). The days of Unleavened Bread recall that the Israelites when they left Egypt had no time to leaven the dough when baking bread (*Exodus* 12). The passover feast celebrates God's gift of freedom.

**vv.13-15** This speech of Jesus shows foreknowledge of what will happen when two of the disciples, who are unnamed, are sent into the city. Luke identifies the disciples as Peter and John (*Luke* 22:8). Presumably they are leaving from Bethany and walking into Jerusalem as Jesus had done on the previous days. Similar foreknowledge had also been demonstrated when Jesus on his approach to Jerusalem had sent two disciples to fetch a colt (*Mark* 11:2).

Jesus asks for a 'guest room', which would be a place where visitors could sleep at night. The same word (*katalyma* in Greek) is found in Luke 2:7, when there is 'no room at the inn'. Jesus then refers to the room as 'a large room upstairs'.

**v.16** It seems that the disciples themselves prepare the meal. One wonders whether they were accompanied by the women disciples.

# The Coming Betrayal

**v.17** The passover meal does not begin until after sunset. Jesus is accompanied by the Twelve, and perhaps by others.

**v.18** Customary depictions of the Last Supper have the disciples seated on one side of a long table with Jesus at the centre. This verse, translated literally, would read 'and when they had lain down'. We should imagine the disciples lying on carpets around a low table using cushions to support themselves. The Aramaic word 'Amen' is used by Jesus to introduce a solemn statement about betrayal by one of the twelve. It is a poignant scene, and brings to mind the words of Psalm 41:9: 'Even my bosom friend in whom I trusted, who ate of my bread, has lifted the heel against me.'

**vv.19-20** As the disciples express disbelief, Jesus reaffirms that one of those sharing the meal will betray him. In the synoptic gospels Jesus does not identify his betrayer to the other disciples. By contrast, in John's gospel, Jesus identifies his betrayer by offering a morsel to Judas (*John* 13:26). At that point Jesus sends Judas out into the night.

**v.21** Jesus once again refers to himself as 'the Son of Man' and speaks of his coming death. He goes 'as it is written of him', for, as Paul writes, 'Christ died for our sins in accordance with the scriptures.' (1 *Corinthians* 15:3) He then says 'woe to that one by whom the Son of Man is betrayed!' Is this a final attempt to change Judas' heart? Or an expression of resigned sadness at the betrayal, accompanied by steadfastness to face the future?

*St Cyprian, bishop of Carthage in the middle of the third century, writes about the patience of Jesus, especially in facing his passion and death:*

*His wonderful patience is seen in the way he dealt with his disciples. He was even able to tolerate Judas to the end with enduring patience. He could eat calmly with his betrayer. He could patiently be aware of his enemy at his own table and not let on. He did not even refuse the kiss of the traitor.*

*(On the Advantage of Patience 6)*

# The Institution of the Eucharist

*There are four accounts of the institution of the Eucharist in the New Testament. The gospel accounts of Mark and Matthew are similar to each other. The gospel account of Luke has similarities with the account of Paul in 1 Corinthians 11:23-25. For instance, both Luke and Paul have the words 'Do this in memory of me.' (Luke 22:19 and 1 Corinthians 11:24), which are not included by Mark and Matthew.*

**v.22** The narrative of the meal does not refer to any of the traditional rituals of the passover meal. In particular, there is no reference at all to the passover lamb. If the ritual of Passover was followed by Jesus, which is by no means certain, the details are being omitted by Mark in order to emphasise the importance of Jesus' new action. The two miracles of the loaves earlier in the gospel of Mark anticipated his actions, when Jesus took the bread, blessed it, broke it and gave it (*Mark* 6:41 and 8:6). The words 'This is my body', expressing Jesus' gift of himself, have been scrutinised and analysed throughout the history of the Church, particularly in debate about the Eucharist. Speaking in Aramaic, Jesus probably used the word *bisra*, meaning 'flesh' and evoking human life in its fragility and weakness. Luke's account adds to the words 'This is my body' the explanatory phrase 'which is given for you' (*Luke* 22:19) The essence of the Eucharist is Christ's self-giving love.

**vv.23-24** In taking the cup with the words 'This is my blood' Jesus once again gives the totality of himself. The blood suggests blood poured out in death and once again emphasises human vulnerability. In speaking of 'my blood of the covenant' Jesus relates his own action to God's covenant with Israel, which was solemnly ratified on Mount Sinai with the blood of animals (*Exodus* 24). Luke has Jesus speak of a 'new covenant', an idea found in Jeremiah 31, which expresses a hopeful, new stage in the relations between God and the people (*Luke* 22:20). The blood of Jesus is 'poured out for many', reminding us of Jesus' words earlier in the gospel that 'the Son of Man came to give his life a ransom for many' (10:45). The word 'many' has an inclusive sense, so that the prayer of consecration over the cup at Mass reads: 'It will be shed for you and for all.'

**v.25** Jesus' words in this verse underline that this is his last meal. The solemnity of the statement is once again emphasised by 'Truly' which translates the Aramaic word 'Amen'. Jesus is saying farewell to the disciples until they are reunited in the kingdom of God. The verse shows that the Eucharist is also an anticipation of life with God. Matthew stresses the community dimension when Jesus says he will drink the fruit of the vine again 'with you' in the kingdom (*Matthew* 26:29). Towards the end of the Book of Revelation an angel says to the visionary: 'Write this: Blessed are those who are invited to the marriage supper of the lamb.' (*Revelation* 19:9) These words we hear in the preparation for Holy Communion.

St Justin Martyr, defender of the Christian faith in the second century, speaks of the early Christian practice of celebrating the Eucharist:

*We do not receive these things as common bread or common drink; but, just as Jesus Christ our Saviour being incarnate by God's Word took flesh and blood for our salvation, so also we have been taught that the food consecrated by the word of prayer which comes from him, from which our flesh and blood are nourished by transformation, is the flesh and blood of that incarnate Jesus. For the apostles in the memoirs composed by them, which are called Gospels, handed down what was commanded them: that Jesus, taking bread and having given thanks, said, "Do this in remembrance of me. This is my body"; and similarly taking the cup and giving thanks he said, "This is my blood"; and gave it to them alone.*

*(First Apology 66)*

The Cenacle in Jerusalem, traditional place of the Last Supper. It is above the tomb of David on Mount Sion.

# The Abandonment by the Disciples

**v.26** 'When they had sung the hymn' is often interpreted as reference to the Hallel psalms of praise which concluded the passover meal. If the Last Supper took place, as is traditionally believed, in the vicinity of Mount Zion, Jesus and his disciples descended into the Kidron valley in order to reach the Mount of Olives.

**v.27** Mark's account of the night before Jesus died is very sober. It is punctuated by reports of the failure of the disciples. As they approach the Mount of Olives Jesus, who had already foretold the betrayal by Judas, now foretells his abandonment by the rest of the disciples. 'You will all become deserters' is the translation given for what is literally 'you will all be scandalized'. A 'scandal' (*skandalon* in Greek) is something which makes people fall, an obstacle which impedes belief. Jesus foresees that his arrest and being treated as a criminal will undermine the faith of the disciples, just as Paul will later write that the crucified Messiah is a 'scandal' or 'stumbling-block' for the Jews (1 *Corinthians* 1:23). Jesus goes on to quote from the prophet Zechariah: 'I will strike the shepherd, and the sheep will be scattered' (*Zechariah* 13:7). This prophet tells of the fate of a mysterious shepherd whose sufferings are understood as foreshadowing those of Jesus.

**v.28** Almost unnoticed amid the negative statements, Jesus once again affirms his belief in his own resurrection and in meeting the disciples again. There will be a reversal of the scattering of the disciples as the risen Jesus gathers them again and restores their faith. The young man at the tomb in 16:7 also promises that the disciples will meet Jesus again in Galilee.

**vv.29-30** Peter insists that he will not fail, but Jesus replies with another solemn 'Amen' statement foreseeing Peter's denials before the cock crows twice. Matthew and Luke omit reference to the cock crowing twice, perhaps because they consider it irrelevant, but reports of cocks crowing repeatedly from the early hours might suggest Mark's account is more accurate.

**v.31** Peter remains adamant that he will not fail Jesus. He uses a Greek word for 'to die with' someone. The Christians in Rome after the martyrdom of Peter, for whom it is thought this gospel was written, would be well aware that despite his infidelity on the night of Jesus' arrest he did eventually 'die with' Christ. Mark underlines that all the other disciples said the same thing.

*Fr Marie-Joseph Lagrange, the great Dominican biblical scholar, founded the Biblical School (Ecole Biblique) in Jerusalem, and lived there for many years. In his commentary on Mark he says:*

*In Jerusalem at the end of March and beginning of April you hear the cock crowing at about 3 o'clock and at about 5.30 in the morning.*

The Kiss of Judas, Scenes from the Life of Christ (mosaic) by Byzantine School, (6th century)

## The Word Lives On

The narrative of the Last Supper as found in Mark is, along with Paul's account in 1 Corinthians 11, very ancient. Matthew's gospel seems to have used Mark as a source and edited the material according to his style and theology. Matthew, for example, accentuates the role of Judas, and has Judas speak the words 'Surely not I, Rabbi?' (26:25), words which are not found in Mark. To Mark's version of the words of Jesus over the cup, Matthew makes the addition that the covenant blood is poured out for many 'for the forgiveness of sins' (26:28). Such subtle changes help us to see the nuances of each gospel. Luke's version of the Last Supper has major differences, and is not reliant on Mark's story.

## In the Lectionary

The narrative of the Last Supper is solemnly read as part of the Passion on Palm Sunday. Mark's account is read in year B. On Maundy Thursday the gospel is that of the washing of the feet, taken from John 13. The abundance of biblical texts appropriate for Holy Week means that much material is not read publicly each year. On the Solemnity of Corpus Christi in Year B verses 12-16 and 22-26 of our text, the preparation for the Passover and the institution of the Eucharist, are read. The verses referring to Judas' betrayal and the abandonment by the disciples are not appropriate for the feast.

The Last Supper by Clive Uptton

# Live the Word of God

**Listen again to the reading: Mark 14:12-31**

**What do you hear now?**
*Suggestions for reflection and prayer*

**What strikes you about Mark's story of the Last Supper?**

**Reflect on the words of St Cyprian about the patience of Jesus given earlier in the commentary.**

**How can we ensure that our participation in Christ's supper does not become empty routine?**

**The Eucharist is the great farewell gift of Jesus to his friends.**
- ❖ Pray that the Eucharist may teach us about the love of God, challenge us to live in self-giving rather than self-serving ways, and fill us with anticipation for the wedding-feast of the Lamb.

**As the Passover celebrates the freedom of God's people, the Eucharist celebrates the new life won for us by Jesus.**
- ❖ May we use our freedom in selfless service, sharing the life of God with all.

**The Last Supper is punctuated by references to the failure of his disciples.**
- ❖ Pray that we may honestly confront our own infidelities and betrayals and strive to correct them.

**'To receive in truth the Body and Blood of Christ given up for us, we must recognize Christ in the poorest, his brothers and sisters.' (Catechism 1397)**
- ❖ May we always remember that the Mass we celebrate is a sending forth in service to those in greatest need.

**Reflect**

*The 'Didache' or 'Teaching of the Twelve Apostles', written about 100, contains the following prayer about the Eucharist:*

*As this fragment of bread was scattered upon the mountains and was gathered to become one, so may your church be gathered together from the ends of the earth into your kingdom.*

*(Didache 9)*

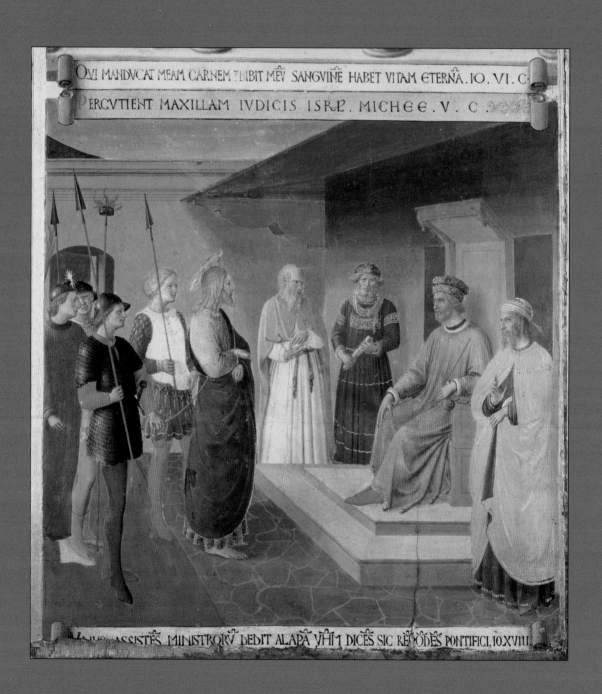

# Hear the Word of God

## Read Mark 14:53-72

53 They took Jesus to the high priest; and all the chief priests, the elders, and the scribes were assembled. 54 Peter had followed him at a distance, right into the courtyard of the high priest; and he was sitting with the guards, warming himself at the fire.

55 Now the chief priests and the whole council were looking for testimony against Jesus to put him to death; but they found none. 56 For many gave false testimony against him, and their testimony did not agree. 57 Some stood up and gave false testimony against him, saying, 58 'We heard him say, 'I will destroy this temple that is made with hands, and in three days I will build another, not made with hands.' ' 59 But even on this point their testimony did not agree.

60 Then the high priest stood up before them and asked Jesus, 'Have you no answer? What is it that they testify against you?' 61 But he was silent and did not answer. Again the high priest asked him, 'Are you the Messiah, the Son of the Blessed One?'

62 Jesus said, 'I am; and 'you will see the Son of Man seated at the right hand of the Power,' and 'coming with the clouds of heaven.' '

63 Then the high priest tore his clothes and said, 'Why do we still need witnesses? 64 You have heard his blasphemy! What is your decision?' All of them condemned him as deserving death. 65 Some began to spit on him, to blindfold him, and to strike him, saying to him, 'Prophesy!' The guards also took him over and beat him.

66 While Peter was below in the courtyard, one of the servant-girls of the high priest came by. 67 When she saw Peter warming himself, she stared at him and said, 'You also were with Jesus, the man from Nazareth.' 68 But he denied it, saying, 'I do not know or understand what you are talking about.' And he went out into the forecourt. Then the cock crowed. 69 And the servant-girl on seeing him, began again to say to the bystanders, 'This man is one of them.' 70 But again he denied it. Then after a little while the bystanders again said to Peter, 'Certainly you are one of them; for you are a Galilean.' 71 But he began to curse, and he swore an oath, 'I do not know this man you are talking about.'

72 At that moment the cock crowed for the second time. Then Peter remembered that Jesus had said to him, 'Before the cock crows twice, you will deny me three times.' And he broke down and wept.

Facing page: Christ Before Caiaphas, detail from the Silver Treasury of Santissima Annunziata, c. 1450-53 by Fra Angelico, (c.1387-1455).

# Understand the Word of God

**This session will explore:**

- ❖ the trial of Jesus before the Sanhedrin
- ❖ the accusations against Jesus
- ❖ the condemnation of Jesus
- ❖ Peter's denials and repentance
- ❖ the message for today.

## Setting in the Gospel

The Passion Narrative in Mark's gospel began with the account of the Last Supper. During the walk to the Garden of Gethsemane Jesus foretold his abandonment by the disciples and the denials by Peter. Mark then gave a portrayal of the anguish of Jesus as he prayed in the garden: 'He began to be distressed and agitated.' (14:33). He gives an honest account of the failure of the disciples to stay awake with Jesus (14:37-41). Judas then arrived, accompanied by 'a crowd with swords and clubs, from the chief priests, the scribes, and the elders' (14:43). Jesus is arrested and the disciples flee, as does the unidentified young man who abandons his linen cloth and runs away naked (14:52).

Our text is located at the house of the high priest. The Jewish trial takes place there, while Peter's denials happen in the courtyard of the house. Jesus is condemned and abandoned, and finally disowned by the disciple he had specially chosen. The objective of the Jewish religious leaders to have Jesus killed, stated at the beginning of the Passion Narrative in 14:1, is being achieved.

# What Kind of Text?

The Passion Narrative in Mark continues to provide a detailed account of the events leading up to the death of Jesus. The material seeks to tell us both what happened and why it happened.

The text of the trial before the Sanhedrin, the court of the Jewish religious leaders presided over by the high priest, raises many questions. The evangelist records the accusations against Jesus but makes it clear that they are false. Jesus is being condemned on trumped up charges by dishonest witnesses. The fact that the trial takes place at night, as is implied by Mark, adds to the sense that this is an irregular process, as indeed does the location of the meeting at the house of the high priest. The evangelist leaves no doubt that Jesus is a victim of gross injustice.

The account of Peter's denials also has a dramatic side to it. There is a developing climax as the maid addresses Peter, and then the bystanders, and the bystanders then address Peter. At each point Peter denies all knowledge of Jesus and the vehemence of his denial increases. While Jesus under trial speaks the truth in the face of falsehood, Peter speaks falsehood in the face of the truth. When Peter hears the cock crow, he breaks down and weeps.

# Commentary: verse by verse reading

## The Arrival at the High Priest's House

*The Pontifical Biblical Commission teaches:*

*The arrest of Jesus, followed by condemnation and death, is the work of the nation's ruling class at that time. Mark regularly opposes the attitude of the leaders to that of 'the crowd' or 'the people', who are favourably disposed to Jesus. Three times the evangelist notes that in their attempts to have Jesus killed, the authorities were inhibited by fear of the people's reaction. Nevertheless, at the end of the trial before Pilate, the chief priests succeeded in sufficiently inciting the attendant crowd to make them choose Barabbas in preference to Jesus. The final decision of Pilate, powerless to calm the crowd, is to 'satisfy' them, which, for Jesus, means crucifixion. This merely incidental crowd certainly cannot be confused with the Jewish people of that time, and even less with the Jews of every age. It should be said that they represent rather the sinful world of which we are all a part.*

*(The Jewish People and their Sacred Scriptures in the Christian Bible, 72)*

**v.53** Those sent to arrest Jesus came from the high priests, elders and scribes, the members of the Sanhedrin. This Jewish council had certain limited powers in this time of Roman occupation. It was the high priest, as the leading Jewish religious and political figure, who presided over the Sanhedrin. Mark states that all the members of the Sanhedrin gathered to interrogate Jesus. In his account of the proceedings, Matthew identifies the high priest as Joseph Caiaphas, who held office from 18 to 36 AD (*Matthew* 26:57).

**v.54** The reference to Peter prepares for the story of his denials. Mark even suggests courage on the part of Peter, since he risks entering the court-yard of the high priest's house. As Fr Lagrange points out in his commentary, the reference to Peter warming himself by the fire is entirely plausible due to the cold spring nights in Palestine.

Christ before the High Priest Gerrit van Honthorst 1592-1656. The candle focuses light upon the face of Christ, the face and raised finger of the High Priest and the book before him. The drama lies in the confrontation of the law, represented by the book, and the Christ.

# Jesus on Trial

**v.55** Mark declares that it is the intention of the gathering to have Jesus killed, and for the first time uses the Greek term *sunedrion*, which gives us the word 'Sanhedrin'. As early as chapter 3 Mark told us that there were those who conspired to destroy Jesus. The Sanhedrin, which now seeks evidence against him, does not have the power to put Jesus to death, as is clear from the words of the Jews to Pilate in John 18:31, 'We are not permitted to put anyone to death'. After the trial before the Sanhedrin, accusations against Jesus will be laid before Pontius Pilate.

**v.56** The evangelist describes the witnesses as 'giving false testimony', which is then compounded by stating that 'their testimony did not agree'. Mark seems to be ridiculing the whole procedure. He implies that no convincing testimony is possible to substantiate a charge against Jesus.

**vv.57-59** The charge brought by the witnesses concerns the destruction of the temple. They claim that Jesus said 'I will destroy this temple that is made with hands, and in three days I will build another not made with hands.' When he left the temple in chapter 13 Jesus said: 'Not one stone will be left here upon another; all will be thrown down.' The cleansing of the temple in chapter 11 might also have encouraged the impression that he was against the temple. When he spoke of the destruction of the temple, Jesus was in fact taking up and developing a theme found in the prophets (*Jeremiah* 7:14 26:6), but he did not threaten that he himself would destroy it. The idea of a 'heavenly temple' not built with human hands is found in Jewish thought of Jesus' time, and in the New Testament Book of Revelation (*Revelation* 21:10).

**vv.60-61** The high priest's challenge is met with silence from Jesus. For Mark Jesus behaves like the suffering servant of the Lord in the book of Isaiah. Isaiah 53:7 reads: 'He was oppressed, and he was afflicted, yet he did not open his mouth; like a lamb that is led to the slaughter, and like a sheep that before its shearers is silent, so he did not open his mouth.' The high priest suddenly introduces a new issue, the identity of Jesus: 'Are you the Messiah, the Son of the Blessed One?'

**v.62** This second issue, the accusation that Jesus claimed to be the Messiah, arises also in the questioning of Jesus by Pilate, which is found in all four gospels. The reply usually given by Jesus to the question about his messianic identity, whether asked by the high priest or by Pilate, is evasive. When Pilate asks Jesus 'Are you the King of the Jews?' Jesus replies 'You say so.' (15:2)

Our present verse is the only one where Jesus gives an unequivocal 'I am' in reply. It is clear from the diversity of the accounts in the gospels that we cannot establish the precise words of these dialogues. Did Jesus solemnly proclaim his true mission at this point? Or did he in fact continue to evade the question, as is suggested by Matthew 26:64, because he was concerned about the misinterpretation of such a claim? We cannot know for sure.

Jesus' reply contains allusion to two biblical texts. We have seen already how Jesus uses words from Daniel 7:13 in Mark 13:26. He uses the same text again here, in a slightly different form. Jesus declares: 'You will see the Son of Man seated at the right hand of the Power, and coming with the clouds of heaven.' Jesus is speaking of his triumph over death and of his return in glory. On this occasion, however, he adds to the Daniel text the statement that he will be 'seated at the right hand of the Power'. This seems to be an allusion to Psalm 110, which describes the messianic king sitting at the right hand of God.

**vv.63-64** It was customary for those engaged in a trial against blasphemy to tear their clothes in outrage. The words of Jesus give the high priest the pretext for a charge of blasphemy, which according to the book of Leviticus (24:16) should be punished by death. The aim of the gathering has been achieved. A false trial with false witnesses reaches a false outcome. The Sanhedrin will present Jesus to Pilate as deserving death.

**v.65** Physical abuse of Jesus follows. Once again Mark seems to be using material about the servant from the book of Isaiah. There are similarities here with the third poem of the servant (*Isaiah* 50:6). Jesus is taunted as a prophet, which reminds us of his fundamental role, to speak words of love and truth.

*St Justin the Martyr writes:*

*The prophets foretold two comings of Christ – one, which has already happened, when he comes in the form of a dishonoured and dying man, and the second, when, as has been foretold, he will come from heaven in glory.*

*(First Apology 52)*

*The Jewish law-code known as the Mishnah, which was compiled at the end of the second century AD, reads as follows:*

*The judges stand up on their feet and rend their garments, and they may not mend them again.*

*(Tractate Sanhedrin 7:5)*

# Peter's Denials

**v.66** While Jesus under trial testifies to the truth and is punished, Peter denies the truth and escapes. He is 'below in the courtyard', showing us that the trial of Jesus probably took place in a large upper room of the high priest's house.

**vv.67-68** The servant girl stares at Peter. She looks intently at him. Peter's stuttering reply shows he is taken by surprise. Mark tells us he leaves the courtyard and goes towards the 'forecourt' or 'porch'. The reference to the first crowing of the cock is not found in some important ancient copies of Mark's gospel, and there is no reference to it in Matthew and Luke. It may well be that an editor of Mark's gospel has added the phrase 'then the cock crowed' to make the fulfilment of Jesus' earlier words to Peter that the cock would crow twice more obvious.

**v.69** Mark's account has the same servant girl speak to Peter again, while Matthew and Luke suggest it is someone different (*Matthew* 26:71 *Luke* 22:58). The danger for Peter increases as the girl tells those standing by: 'This man is one of them'.

**v.70** After Peter's second denial the danger increases further, for the bystanders themselves take up the accusation. He is recognised as a Galilean, probably due to his accent or dialect.

**v.71** The extreme danger in which Peter finds himself leads him to panic, to curse and to swear. He completely disowns Jesus with the words 'I do not know this man.'

**v.72** Jesus' words are fulfilled as the cock crows for the second time. Each of the synoptic evangelists spells out the precise words of Jesus which predicted Peter's denials. Mark ends with the powerful statement that Peter 'broke down and wept'.

*St John Chrysostom reflects on the honesty of the evangelist:*

*In this respect we most marvel at Mark, because not only did he refuse to hide Peter's fault, but wrote the account of it in greater detail than the others.*

*(The Gospel of Matthew 85.1)*

*From a homily of St Jerome:*

*When he lacked the power of the Spirit, Saint Peter trembled at the voice of a maid-servant. With the power of the Spirit, he withstood princes and kings.*

*(Homily 65)*

Peter denies Christ,
Italian School, (15th century)

Peter's denial as viewed through
the eyes of an African culture:
Peter's Denial by Mafu Christian
community of North Cameroon
(1973)

## The Word Lives On

Each gospel gives an account of an interrogation of Jesus by the Jewish leaders. While Mark and Matthew report that this happened at night, Luke tells us that it happened the following morning (*Luke* 22:66). Luke makes no reference to the charge of destroying the temple, and the principal issue for all three synoptic gospels is whether Jesus claims to be the Messiah. In John's gospel there is no detailed reference to the charges against Jesus at this point.

All four gospels report Peter's denials. In Luke's gospel the denials are naturally reported before the interrogation of Jesus the following morning. Despite his custom of putting less emphasis on the failure of the apostles, Luke still faithfully records the tradition. He does however omit all reference to Peter's cursing and swearing. Most poignantly, Luke tells us that, when the cock crows, Jesus turns and looks at Peter, so that Peter realises that he has betrayed Jesus (*Luke* 22:61). In John's gospel the story of the denials is interrupted by the questioning of Jesus by Annas, former high priest and father-in-law of Caiaphas, the high priest in office at the time.

Peter Went Out and Wept Bitterly, illustration for 'The Life of Christ' c. 1886-94 by James Jacques Joseph Tissot, (1836-1902)

## In the Lectionary

The narrative of the trial of Jesus and the denials of Peter in the Gospel of Mark is solemnly read as part of the Passion on Palm Sunday in Year B.

# Live the Word of God

**Listen again to the reading: Mark 14:53-72**

**What do you hear now?**

*Suggestions for reflection and prayer*

**What features of Mark's description of Jesus and of Peter stand out for you?**

**Reflect on the words of St Jerome given in the commentary about the power of the Spirit in the life of Peter.**

**How important is it to honour the truth in our daily lives?**

**Jesus speaks the truth, even when his life is threatened.**

❖ Pray for the courage and strength to speak the truth, especially when we are tempted to collude with what is wrong, and when our standing with others may suffer.

**Peter fails out of fear that he might share the fate of Jesus**

❖ Pray for courage to face whatever trials may come from fidelity to Christ. Pray for those persecuted for their faith in many regions of the world today.

**Peter breaks down and weeps.**

❖ Pray that we may have the strength to recognise those things in our lives which need to change, those things which are in conflict with integrity of faith.

**Peter receives the compassionate forgiveness of Jesus.**

❖ Pray for the gift of compassion for those who seem unable to confront the problems of their lives.

*St Gregory the Great uses the story of Peter's denials to give a lesson about compassion:*

*Here we must ask ourselves: why did almighty God permit the one he had placed over the whole church to be frightened by the voice of a maid-servant, and even to deny Christ himself? This we know was a great dispensation of the divine mercy, so that he who was to be the shepherd of the church might learn through his own fall to have compassion on others. God therefore first shows him to himself, and then places him over others. He learns through his own weakness how to bear mercifully with the weakness of others.*

*(Homilies on the Gospels 21)*

# Jesus Crucified

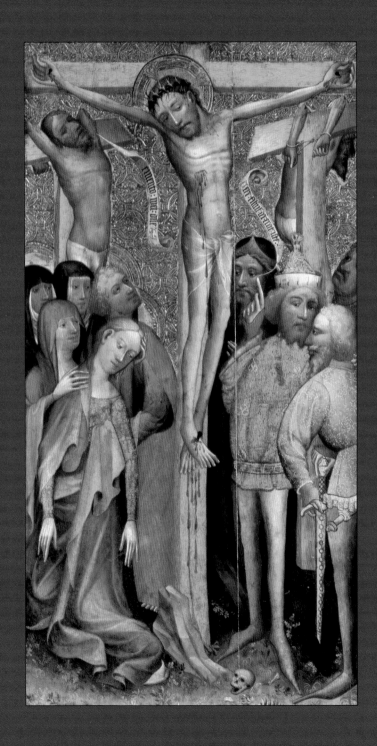

# Hear the Word of God

## Read Mark 15:21-39

21 They compelled a passer-by, who was coming in from the country to carry his cross; it was Simon of Cyrene, the father of Alexander and Rufus.

22 They brought Jesus to the place called Golgotha (which means the place of a skull).

23 And they offered him wine mixed with myrrh; but he did not take it. 24 And they crucified him, and divided his clothes among them, casting lots to decide what each should take.

25 It was nine o'clock in the morning when they crucified him. 26 The inscription of the charge against him read, 'The King of the Jews.' 27 And with him they crucified two bandits, one on his right and one on his left.

29 Those who passed by derided him, shaking their heads and saying, 'Aha! You who would destroy the temple and build it in three days. 30 Save yourself, and come down from the cross!' 31 In the same way the chief priests, along with the scribes, were also mocking him among themselves and saying, 'He saved others; he cannot save himself. 32 Let the Messiah, the King of Israel, come down from the cross now, so that we may see and believe.' Those who were crucified with him also taunted him.

33 When it was noon, darkness came over the whole land until three o'clock in the afternoon.

34 At three o'clock Jesus cried out with a loud voice, '*Eloi, Eloi, lema sabachthani*?' which means, 'My God, my God, why have you forsaken me?'

35 When some of the bystanders heard it, they said, 'Listen, he is calling for Elijah.'

36 And someone ran, filled a sponge with sour wine, put it on a stick, and gave it to him to drink, saying, 'Wait, let us see whether Elijah will come to take him down.'

37 Then Jesus gave a loud cry and breathed his last.

38 And the curtain of the temple was torn in two, from top to bottom.

39 Now when the centurion, who stood facing him, saw that in this way he breathed his last, he said, 'Truly this man was God's Son!'

Facing page: The Crucifixion, c 1395 by the English School.

# Understand the Word of God

**This session will explore:**

- ❖ the journey of Jesus to Golgotha
- ❖ the crucifixion
- ❖ the mockery of Jesus
- ❖ the death of Jesus
- ❖ the message for today.

## Setting in the Gospel

Mark reported the trial before the Sanhedrin and the denials of Peter on the night Jesus had been arrested in Gethsemane. The following morning Jesus is handed over for interrogation to Pontius Pilate, the Roman governor. Pilate questions Jesus about his identity, and Jesus answers in an evasive way (15:2). The religious leaders incite the crowd to ask for the release of the criminal Barabbas, so that Pilate accedes to the pressure from the crowd to have Jesus executed (15:15).

Jesus undergoes the customary scourging inflicted by the Romans on those condemned to crucifixion (15:15), and suffers further abuse from the soldiers who take advantage of the messianic claims made for him to insult him further with purple cloak, crown of thorns and mock salutations (15:16-19). In their mockery of him the Roman soldiers unwittingly proclaim the truth that he is the 'King of the Jews'. It is at this point that our text takes up the story with the journey of Jesus to the place of execution.

Mark's Passion Narrative is reaching its climax.

# What Kind of Text?

The Passion Narrative in Mark continues to provide a detailed account of the events leading to the death of Jesus. In these verses we follow the 'way of the cross', as Jesus carries his cross to the place of death. Mark's presentation is full of incidents, and he sometimes provides extraordinary detail, such as the information about the sons of Simon of Cyrene, which Matthew omits. Mark has also structured the account by reference to the time of the day, speaking of the third hour (nine o'clock), the sixth hour (noon), and the ninth hour (three o'clock).

Christ Mocked, by Dutch artist Hieronymus Bosch (1460-1516). The contemporary setting invites awareness of mockery and cynicism for Christ in every age.

The account begins and ends with individuals who seem well-disposed to Jesus, Simon who assists Jesus in carrying his cross, and the centurion who reacts positively to the death of Jesus. Between the references to these two men we have three groups who show a negative attitude to Jesus, the passers-by, the chief priests and the scribes, and the criminals crucified with Jesus. Mark seems to know nothing of Luke's tradition of the 'good thief'.

The text of Mark is packed with detail, illustrating how the death of Jesus occurs amid the ordinariness of life. And yet the way Jesus dies, and the subsequent unexplained tearing of the temple veil, point to the unique significance of what is narrated here.

# Commentary: verse by verse reading

## The way to Golgotha

*Crucifixion was an atrocious form of punishment, reserved by the Romans for slaves and foreigners guilty of serious crimes. Roman citizens were generally not crucified. The victims would be crucified outside the walls of the town and left to suffer from hunger, dehydration, dogs and vultures. The Roman writer Tacitus reports how in the persecution of the emperor Nero Christians suffered crucifixion: they were covered with wild beasts' skins and torn to death by dogs; or they were fastened on crosses and, when daylight faded, were burned to serve as lamps by night. (Annals 15.44.4)*

*The location of Calvary is to be found within the Church of the Holy Sepulchre, built by the emperor Constantine in the fourth century. While the basilica now lies inside the medieval walls of Jerusalem, in the time of Jesus the location was outside the walls. At the beginning of the first century the site was a disused quarry, which had become a place for burials. It was in this vicinity that the crucifixion and burial of Jesus took place. The early Christians held liturgical celebrations at the site, and the emperor Constantine had a church commemorating the Resurrection built in the same place.*

**v.21** Despite the customary artistic portrayals of Jesus carrying his cross, it is generally understood that what Jesus actually carried was the cross-beam (known by the Latin term *patibulum*), which would be attached to the vertical part of the cross on arrival at the place of execution. The fact that Jesus needed assistance in carrying the cross suggests the severity of the scourging inflicted by the Romans in preparation for crucifixion. By forcing Simon to assist Jesus the Roman soldiers ensured that Jesus did not die before reaching the place of execution. Mark alone tells us that Simon of Cyrene was the father of Alexander and Rufus. Cyrene lies in north Africa, but why should the two sons of Simon be mentioned here? Some have speculated that Simon and his two sons subsequently became Christians.

**v.22** The name 'Golgotha' is derived from the Aramaic word for 'skull', presumably because the place which bore the name was shaped like a skull. Our word 'Calvary' is derived from the Latin word *calvaria*, also meaning 'skull', which is found in the Latin version of the gospel.

**v.23** The attempted offering of wine mixed with myrrh is an action of kindness intended to alleviate suffering. In the book of Proverbs we read: 'Give strong drink to one who is perishing, and wine to those in bitter distress.' (*Proverbs* 31:6) Wine was often spiced with myrrh in ancient times. Jesus does not accept the offer of wine intended to reduce his suffering.

The devotion known as the via crucis or the 'Stations of the Cross' is well-known to Catholics. It emerged from the desire of Christians to follow the path of Jesus to the cross, something which could otherwise only be done by pilgrims visiting the Holy Land. The stations may be of stone, wood, or metal, sculptured or carved, painted or engraved, but occasionally simple wooden crosses are erected. They are generally found around the interior walls of a church, though often

Christ Carrying the Cross, c. 1651 by Eustache Le Sueur, (1617-55)

Stations of the cross along the Via Dolorosa, Jerusalem.

they are outside. In the history of the devotion the number of stations varied but the number was eventually fixed at fourteen. Not all of the stations are found in the gospel Passion accounts. The additional stations fill out the story of Jesus' passion and death.

# The Crucifixion of Jesus

**v.24** The act of crucifixion seems to have entailed nailing of the wrists to the cross-beam which the victim had carried to the place of execution. The cross-beam was then fixed to the upright beam, which already stood in the ground at the site of execution. Finally the feet were nailed to the upright beam. Sometimes victims were tied to the cross, but reference to the wounds of the nails in Luke 24:39 and John 20:25 points to the crucifixion of Jesus by nailing. The stripping of Jesus raises the question whether Jesus was crucified naked, as was often the custom, or whether, perhaps due to Jewish sensitivities concerning nakedness, Jesus still wore a loincloth. Mark's account of the crucifixion invites us to contemplate it in all its horror. The sharing out of the garments of the victim was common practice. Christians would make connections with Psalm 22:18, which reads: 'they divide my clothes among themselves, and for my clothing they cast lots.'

**v.25** Only Mark has three references to the timing of events. The Greek text of the gospel informs us that Jesus was crucified 'at the third hour'. This refers to nine o'clock in the morning, and is in conflict with what is recorded in John 19:14, that Jesus was still in the presence of Pilate 'at the sixth hour', which is midday. This discrepancy reflects the different ways in which the story of Jesus' death developed. Mark will also refer to 'the sixth hour' and 'the ninth hour', and it may be that his presentation of the events on the day of Jesus' death reflects Christian times of prayer rather than accurate historical information.

**v.26** The gospels record that the charge against Jesus was fixed to the cross. Mark tells us that the charge simply gave the basic accusation 'The king of the Jews'. This part of the story is most developed in John 19:19-22.

**v.27** Jesus is not crucified alone, but with two 'bandits'. The Greek term used here, *lestes*, refers to outlaws, those who use arms to attack and plunder. The traditional reference to 'thieves' is not broad enough, and Mark has no knowledge of the story of the 'good thief' reported in Luke 23:39-43.

**v.28** See margin.

*Verse 28*

*There is no verse 28 in our text. The verse is found in a very few ancient manuscripts of this gospel. It reads: 'And the scripture was fulfilled that says: And he was counted among the lawless.' The most reliable and most ancient copies of Mark's gospel do not contain these words, which were probably added to some copies of Mark in later times by scribes who wanted to show the relevance of these words from Isaiah 53:12 to what is being reported.*

## Jesus derided

**vv.29-30** Jesus is derided by three different groups. Passers-by approaching the city or leaving it use Jesus' reported threats against the temple to mock him. This recalls the first accusation made against Jesus in the trial before the Sanhedrin (14:58).

**vv.31-32** The chief priests and scribes are the second group. They mock Jesus among themselves. They allude to the second accusation brought against Jesus in his trial, his supposed claim to be the Messiah. The priests and scribes are unaware of what God intends, that the Messiah should demonstrate the goodness of God in an altogether unexpected way by accepting death on the cross. Finally, the two men crucified with Jesus join in the mockery of Jesus.

*Isaiah 13:10 reads:*

*For the stars of the heavens and their constellations will not give their light; the sun will be dark at its rising, and the moon will not shed its light.*

*Amos 8:9 reads:*

*On that day, says the Lord God, I will make the sun go down at noon, and darken the earth in broad daylight.*

*The four gospels report seven different speeches of Jesus on the cross, known as the 'seven last words' of Jesus. In addition to the words found in Mark, which are also recorded in Matthew, Luke contains three 'words' of Jesus (Luke 23:34, 43 and 46), and John a further three 'words' (John 19:26-27, 28 and 30).*

# The Death of Jesus

**v.33** Mark's second time reference is to the 'sixth hour', which is noon.

Christians have given various explanations of this darkness at noon. Darkness was associated with the deaths of great men in the Roman and Greek world, but Mark may be alluding to the words of the prophets about darkness on the day of the Lord, as found in Isaiah 13:10 and Amos 8:9.

**v.34** At 'the ninth hour', which is three o'clock, Jesus cries out with the opening words of Psalm 22. The words are recorded in Aramaic. The psalm is a lament of a persecuted just man, and though the psalm concludes on a hopeful note we should take seriously the sense of total abandonment felt by Jesus as he approaches his death.

**vv.35-36** The Aramaic form of the cry of Jesus is misunderstood by the by-standers to be an appeal to Elijah, who, as the prophet expected to return at the end of time, was traditionally thought to help those who were dying. Sour wine, the customary drink of the Roman soldiers, seems to be given to Jesus in an attempt to prolong consciousness.

**v.37** By using the Greek expression which means literally 'he breathed out' the evangelist may be suggesting the willingness of Jesus to give up his life. Matthew will speak of Jesus 'giving up his spirit' (*Matthew 27:50*).

**v.38** The mysterious reference to the tearing of the temple curtain seems to suggest that God, who has kept silence until now, reacts to the death of the Son. This enigmatic verse has been interpreted in various ways by Christians. The destruction of the curtain may suggest that the death of Jesus opens access for all peoples to the dwelling-place of God.

**v.39** That Jesus died for all is now suggested by the reaction of the Roman centurion. People have wondered what the phrase 'son of God' might have meant for the centurion, but his words show he has understood something which others have failed to see. Mark no doubt wishes to conclude the story of Jesus as he began it in 1:1 and 1:11 by affirming the identity of Jesus as the unique and beloved Son of the Father. It is in his death that the true identity of Jesus is revealed as the Son who does the Father's will, and as the Messiah who gives up his life as 'a ransom for many' (*Mark* 10:45).

*St Augustine comments on the freedom with which Christ dies:*

*Those robbers crucified next to him, did they breathe their last when they wanted to? They were held fast by the chains of the flesh because they were not the creators of the flesh. Fastened by nails, they were tormented for a long time because they were not masters of their infirmity. But the Lord took on flesh in the virgin's womb when he wished it. He came forth to humanity when he wished it. He lived in history as long as he wished it. He departed from the flesh when he wished it. This is a sign of power, not of necessity.*

*(Tractates on John 37.9)*

In this depiction of Calvary Dutch artist Rubens focuses on the centurion piercing the side of Jesus to verify his death, reported in John 19:34. The surrounding scene is also shown in some detail.

## The Word Lives On

Mark's rather stark account of the death of Jesus is enriched by Matthew and Luke in their different ways. Matthew speaks of more strange events after the death of Jesus, the shaking of the earth, the splitting of rocks, the opening of tombs, and the resurrection of the saints and their appearance to many (*Matthew* 27:51-53).

Mafu Crucifixion.

The account given by Luke shows awareness of other traditions not reported by Mark and Matthew. Jesus meets the women of Jerusalem (*Luke* 23:27-32). Jesus speaks to the 'good thief' (*Luke* 23:40-43). Luke also records three more of the seven 'last words' of Jesus (*Luke* 23:34, 43 and 46).

## In the Lectionary

Mark's narrative of the death of Jesus is solemnly read as part of the Passion on Palm Sunday in Year B. It is also one of the gospel readings laid down for funeral liturgies.

# Live the Word of God

**Listen again to the reading: Mark 15:21-39**

**What do you hear now?**

*Suggestions for reflection and prayer*

**What parts of Mark's story of the death of Jesus touched you most deeply?**

**Reflect on the words of St Augustine at the end of the commentary.**

**How can we deepen in our minds and hearts the awareness that 'by his wounds we have been healed'?**

**Reflect**

*Christ also suffered for you, leaving you an example, so that you should follow in his steps. He committed no sin, and no deceit was found in his mouth. When he was abused, he did not return abuse; when he suffered, he did not threaten; but he entrusted himself to the one who judges justly. He himself bore our sins in his body on the cross, so that, free from sins, we might live for righteousness; by his wounds you have been healed. For you were going astray like sheep, but now you have returned to the shepherd and guardian of your souls.*

*(1 Peter 2:21-25)*

**Simon is constrained by the Romans to assist Jesus.**

❖ Pray for the acceptance of hardship and the vision to turn suffering into a source of blessing.

**Jesus suffers intense agony, and mocking rejection.**

❖ Pray for true and constant compassion for the sufferings of others, and the courage to diminish rather than add to the pain of the world.

**Jesus cries out to God in total abandonment.**

❖ Pray for honesty in our prayer, and the ability to hear the cries of anguish of others.

**The centurion has the generosity to see what he had not seen.**

❖ Pray for new vision even when it means changing deep-seated ways and opinions.

# Jesus Risen

# Hear the Word of God

## Read Mark 16:1-20

¹ When the sabbath was over, Mary Magdalene, and Mary the mother of James, and Salome bought spices, so that they might go and anoint him. ² And very early on the first day of the week, when the sun had risen, they went to the tomb.

³ They had been saying to one another, 'Who will roll away the stone for us from the entrance to the tomb?' ⁴ When they looked up, they saw that the stone, which was very large, had already been rolled back.

⁵ As they entered the tomb, they saw a young man, dressed in a white robe, sitting on the right side; and they were alarmed. ⁶ But he said to them 'Do not be alarmed; you are looking for Jesus of Nazareth, who was crucified. He has been raised; he is not here. Look, there is the place they laid him. ⁷ But go, tell his disciples and Peter that he is going ahead of you to Galilee; there you will see him, just as he told you.'

⁸ So they went out and fled from the tomb, for terror and amazement had seized them; and they said nothing to anyone, for they were afraid.

⁹ Now after he rose early on the first day of the week, he appeared first to Mary Magdalene, from whom he had cast out seven demons. ¹⁰ She went out and told those who had been with him, while they were mourning and weeping. ¹¹ But when they had heard that he was alive and had been seen by her, they would not believe it.

¹² After this he appeared in another form to two of them, as they were walking into the country. ¹³ And they went back and told the rest, but they did not believe them.

¹⁴ Later he appeared to the eleven themselves as they were sitting at the table; and he upbraided them for their lack of faith and stubbornness, because they had not believed those who saw him after he had risen. ¹⁵ And he said to them, 'Go into all the world and proclaim the good news to the whole creation. ¹⁶ The one who believes and is baptized will be saved; but the one who does not believe will be condemned.'

¹⁷ And these signs will accompany those who believe; by using my name they will cast out demons; they will speak in new tongues; ¹⁸ they will pick up snakes in their hands, and if they drink any deadly thing, it will not hurt them; they will lay their hands on the sick, and they will recover.'

¹⁹ So then the Lord Jesus, after he had spoken to them, was taken up into heaven and sat down at the right hand of God. ²⁰ And they went out and proclaimed the good news everywhere, while the Lord worked with them and confirmed the message by the signs that accompanied it.

Facing page: Icon of the Resurrection in the Orthodox tradition.

# Understand the Word of God

**This session will explore:**

- ❖ the problem of the ending of Mark's gospel
- ❖ the discovery of the empty tomb
- ❖ the appearances of the risen Jesus
- ❖ the message for today.

## Setting in the Gospel

The gospel does not end with the death and burial of Jesus. The story is complete only when the risen Jesus comes to meet his disciples. The preaching about Jesus does not end with Golgotha and the death and burial of Jesus, but with the empty tomb and the appearances of the risen Lord.

Mark chapter 16, like the final chapters of all the gospels, proclaims that Jesus is risen. Like the other gospels, Mark begins with the discovery of the empty tomb (16:1-8). The women who had been present at a distance as Jesus died (15:40) are the same women who, once the sabbath rest is over, go to anoint the body of Jesus. They are amazed to find the stone rolled back and the body of Jesus gone.

What we find next in the Gospel of Mark is quite a puzzle. Whereas the other gospels follow the discovery of the empty tomb of Jesus with detailed narratives of his appearances, either to the women, or to the eleven disciples or to others, the text of Mark in 16:9-20 seems to present a summary of appearances of Jesus found more fully in the other gospels. These final verses display a different style and seem like an appendix, a portion tacked on to the end of the gospel.

# What Kind of Text?

There are two sections in Mark chapter 16. The story of the discovery of the empty tomb contains similar elements to those found in Matthew, Luke and John. The women visit the tomb in order to anoint Jesus. To their amazement the stone has been removed. A young man in white declares that Jesus is risen. But then, unlike in the other gospel accounts, the women flee in fear and tell no-one about what they have seen.

If, as seems the case, these are the final words written by Mark, it is an extraordinary way to end a gospel. Was Mark prevented from finishing his gospel by arrest or sudden illness? Was the final page of the gospel lost?

The second section in the chapter, which is largely a summary of appearances of Jesus narrated in other gospels, brings the gospel to an end on a positive note. This section also contains a particular emphasis on the unwillingness of the disciples to believe what is told them, which leads Jesus to reprimand them for their failure to believe the good news. Jesus also speaks at length about the signs which will be worked by believers.

*A study of the ancient copies of Mark's gospel still available to us adds to the mystery. Among the oldest copies are various parchment books, known as 'codices'. The Codex Sinaiticus, displayed in London's British Library, and the Codex Vaticanus, kept in the Vatican Library in Rome, both date from the fourth century, and neither of these authoritative copies contains vv.9-20. On the other hand, other ancient copies of Mark do have these verses. Verses 9-20 are canonical, which means they are considered to be inspired scripture, but they do not seem to be part of what the evangelist wrote. This distinction is most important. A biblical book, even a gospel, is sometimes the product of more than one author.*

*The Codex Sinaiticus is so called because it was discovered in the Monastery of St Catherine at the foot of Mount Sinai. Dating to the 4th century AD, it contains portions of the Old Testament and the whole of the New Testament. The Codex is like a modern book, and the material used is parchment or vellum, which is made from animal skins. Such books were replacing the less manageable papyrus scrolls. Constantin von Tischendorf, who discovered the manuscript in 1844, described the Codex Sinaiticus as 'the most important manuscript in the whole world, a veritable pillar to sustain divine truth'.*

## Commentary: verse by verse reading
## The Empty Tomb

**v.1** While all the male disciples had fled at Jesus' arrest, some women disciples had stayed to observe from a distance the crucifixion of Jesus (15:40). Mark names three of them: Mary Magdalene, Mary the mother of James and of Joses, and Salome. Two of them are mentioned again at the burial (15:47), and all three as our text begins. It is as if the evangelist is assuring us that they knew where the tomb was, and therefore when the time came they went back to the right place. The tomb now discovered empty is indeed the tomb in which the body of Jesus was placed. The three women intended to perform an anointing of the body of Jesus with their 'spices' which seem to be perfumed ointments, for there had been no time to complete this act of reverence before the sabbath began.

**v.2** All four gospels agree that a group of women went to the tomb early on the sabbath morning.

**vv.3-4** The women have been asking themselves how they might gain access to the tomb, closed as it is by a large stone. Three gospels narrate quite simply that the stone had been removed. It is only in Matthew's gospel that the women witness the removal of the stone by an angel (*Matthew* 28:2). This attempt by Matthew to explain the inexplicable might remind us of how at the death of Jesus Matthew adds references to the quaking of the earth and the splitting of rocks (*Matthew* 27:51).

**v.5** According to Mark, as the women enter the tomb, they see a young man, dressed in white. In Luke's gospel they meet two men. The role of such messengers, sometimes known as 'interpreting angels', is to give a trustworthy explanation of events and visions. The tomb is empty, not because the body has been stolen, but because Jesus has been raised from the dead. Mark tells us that the first reaction of the women is one of alarm. The Greek word translated here as 'they were alarmed' could also be understood as denoting terror.

**v.6** The young man reassures them and gives the true explanation of the empty tomb. The crucified one has been raised from the dead. The young man announces what is the heart of the gospel message: Jesus was crucified, but he has been raised!

**v.7** Awareness of the resurrection leads to mission. The women are to tell the disciples, and Peter. Why does Mark's gospel contain this special reference to Peter? Perhaps the emphasis is intended to rehabilitate Peter after his denials. Perhaps it simply confirms Peter as the first among the disciples. They are to see the risen Jesus in Galilee, as Jesus himself had foreseen earlier in the gospel (14:28). Was it perhaps the intention of Mark to end his gospel with the account of an appearance in Galilee, as Matthew would do (28:16-20)?

**v.8** The failure of the women to proclaim the good news of the resurrection at first sight appears strange. The discovery of the empty tomb was a confusing and disorientating event. It was only after the appearances of the risen Jesus that the truth of the resurrection became irresistibly clear. It may also be true, as some commentators have suggested, that Mark is completing his gospel on an ironic note. Throughout the gospel Jesus had warned his disciples and others not to proclaim the truth about him for fear that messianic fervour would take over and distort his mission. Such people had often disobeyed Jesus' warning. Now that these women are instructed to proclaim the good news about Jesus, they say nothing to anyone due to fear. Proclaiming the good news, Mark infers, is no easy task. Disciples will need courage to preach the gospel.

*The New Testament has various ways of speaking about the resurrection of Jesus. In the Acts of the Apostles we read frequently that 'God raised Jesus' (Acts 3:15 and 4:10). Elsewhere, as here, we read that 'he has been raised', with the implication that the Father raised him from death. In other texts a different Greek word (anistemi rather than egeiro) is used to state that 'Jesus rose from the dead.' The different expressions show how the New Testament authors grappled with the reality of the resurrection and attributed the action sometimes to God and sometimes to Jesus. In John's gospel we read 'I have power to lay down my life and power to take it up again.' (John 10:18)*

# The Ending of the Gospel

The opening prayer of the Mass for the memorial of St Mary Magdalene (July 22nd) reads:

Father, your Son first entrusted to Mary Magdalene the joyful news of his resurrection. By her prayers and example may we proclaim Christ as our living Lord and one day see him in glory.

The disciples are quite reluctant to believe, and unwilling to be deceived. This point is made very strongly in the Gospel of John, when Thomas refuses to accept the testimony of the other disciples, and only believes when he himself sees Jesus. The message is clear: faith is not easy. As Jesus says to Thomas: 'Blessed are those who have not seen and yet have come to believe.' (John 20:29)

**v.9** The additional section of the gospel begins with a new introduction of Mary Magdalene. It is as though she had not been mentioned before. Luke 8:2 also refers to Mary as the one 'from whom seven demons had gone out', a reference to a severe illness of which Jesus had cured her. John chapter 20 contains a full account of an appearance of Jesus to Mary Magdalene.

**vv.10-11** Mary Magdalene is the first bringer of the good news of the resurrection. It is for this that the liturgy of her feast-day honours Mary. The reaction of 'those who had been with him' is one of disbelief. This too is a repeated theme of the resurrection narratives. When, in Luke's gospel, Mary Magdalene and the other women tell the apostles of the empty tomb, Luke writes: 'But these words seemed to them an idle tale, and they did not believe them.' (Luke 24:11)

**vv.12-13** These verses clearly refer to the story of the two disciples on the road to Emmaus narrated in Luke 24:13-35. Interestingly, the text says Jesus appears 'in another form'. The risen Jesus, it seems, is not immediately recognisable by his friends. In John 20:14-16 Magdalene thinks he is the gardener and only gradually recognises Jesus. The evangelists express in this way that Jesus, despite being the same, is also subtly different. The reality of the resurrection and of the risen body is hard to put into words. These verses add to the Emmaus story that the other disciples are unwilling to believe what the Emmaus disciples report. The disciples seem not to be expecting Jesus to rise from the dead and are sceptical of any reports of his appearance.

**v.14** The reporting of the appearance of Jesus to the whole group of the eleven disciples while they are at table recalls the appearance in Luke 24:36-49. But this verse also introduces once more the theme of disbelief, bringing it to a climax as Jesus reprimands the disciples for their lack of faith and stubbornness. The Gospel of Mark contains earlier reprimands of Jesus to the disciples (as in 8:17) but his words were never so harsh.

Left: Christ and Mary Magdalene by Lavina Fontana (1552-1641)

Below: Supper at Emmaus, 1632 by Cryn Hendricks Volmaryn (1604-45)

**vv.15-16** Jesus continues on a more positive note. In words reminiscent of the sending out of the disciples in Matthew 28:19 'Go and make disciples of all nations!' the disciples are sent out in mission to the whole world. Belief and baptism are essential for salvation. The starkness of the choice is apparent. These words reflect the experience of missionary preaching.

**vv.17-18** There follows a list of five 'signs' which will accompany the believer, and perhaps particularly the preacher. The use of the Greek word *semeia*, 'signs', in reference to miraculous healings is unusual in this gospel and another indication of different authorship. The casting out of demons has already been practised by the disciples (*Mark* 6:13). Speaking in tongues is a phenomenon mentioned by Paul, who prizes the gift of prophecy more highly (1 *Corinthians* 14). The handling of snakes recalls the report of Paul's encounter with a viper on the island of Malta (*Acts* 28:3-6). Immunity from drinking poison is promised. A later unreliable tradition attached to apocryphal stories of St John the apostle speaks of John being unharmed when he drank from a poisoned chalice. The imposition of hands for healing is, like exorcism, something already practised by the disciples during Jesus' ministry (*Mark* 6:13).

**v.19** The additions to Mark conclude with a brief reference to the ascension of Jesus, referred to for the first time in the gospel as 'the Lord Jesus'. Other references to the ascension are found in Luke 24:51 and Acts 1:11. Jesus' ascension is expressed in a similar way to the ascension of the prophet Elijah in 2 Kings 2:11. Sitting at the right hand of God recalls the words of Jesus to Caiaphas: 'You will see the Son of Man seated at the right hand of the Power.' (*Mark* 14:62)

**v.20** The concluding verse brings the gospel to an end in a positive way. It summarises what is narrated in detail in the Acts of the Apostles, that the good news was preached everywhere, and extraordinary signs demonstrated the continuing presence of the Lord. This may remind us of the final words of Jesus in the Gospel of Matthew: 'And remember, I am with you always, to the end of the age.' (*Matthew* 28:20)

## The Word Lives On

While the empty tomb story of Mark seems to have been adopted and developed in the gospels of Matthew and Luke, the final verses of Mark 16 are a later account of what is found more fully in other gospels. But these verses also give their own particular emphasis: despite the slowness to believe of the disciples the risen Lord supports their work of preaching and the good news is brought to the peoples of the world.

## In the Lectionary

The text of the empty tomb story is read as the gospel reading at the Easter Vigil in Year B. Mark 16:9-15 is read on the Saturday of Easter Week, once the detailed accounts of resurrection appearances from the other gospels have been read at Mass throughout Easter week. The verses narrating the mission of the disciples and the ascension of Jesus (16:15-20) are read on the Solemnity of the Ascension in Year B.

*St Bede speaks of the abiding presence of Christ:*

*Because he who was taken up into heaven is both God and a human being, he remains on earth with the saints in the humanity which he took from the earth, but equally in the divinity with which he fills earth and heaven all days even to the consummation of the world. From this it is understood that even up to the end, the world will not lack those in whom there will be divine abiding and indwelling. Nor should we doubt that those struggling in this world will deserve to have Christ abiding in their hearts as a guest, and will abide with Christ in his kingdom after the contests of this world.*

*(Homilies on the Gospels 2.8)*

'Go tell ev'ryone the news that God's kingdom has come'
(God's Spirit is in my heart, Alan Dale and Hubert Richards)

# Live the Word of God

*From the Exsultet, the ancient hymn sung at the Easter Vigil:*

*This is the night on which Jesus Christ broke the chains of death and rose triumphant from the grave!*

*What good would life have been to us had Christ not come as our Redeemer? Father, how wonderful your care for us! How boundless your merciful love! To ransom a slave you gave away your Son.*

**Listen again to the reading: Mark 16:1-20**

**What do you hear now?**
*Suggestions for reflection and prayer*

**What strikes you most in Mark's final chapter?**

**Reflect how the words of the Exsultet express the essence of the gospel message.**

**What will you take with you as the message of Mark?**

**The women remain faithful to Christ, even though their response may seem inadequate.**

❖ Pray for an enduring faith that, despite the problems of life and the mysteries we cannot understand, we will be led to truth.

**The gospel shows that the disciples of Jesus were not gullible individuals, ready to accept any rumour about Jesus' resurrection.**

❖ Pray for honesty in our faith, and a deep commitment to the search for truth.

**The disciples take up the call to evangelise and bring the good news to the peoples of the world.**

❖ Pray for vision and new courage to proclaim the good news with clarity and compassion to our own society and to the world, knowing that the Lord is with us always, 'to the end of the age'.

**St Bede says that those struggling in this world deserve to have Christ abiding in their hearts as a guest, and will themselves abide with Christ in his kingdom after the contests of this world.**

❖ Pray for awareness of Christ's presence in word and Sacrament, that we may be signs of hope for the world.

### Reflect

*The Church, then, the one flock of God, like a standard lifted on high for the nations, brings the gospel of peace to all humankind as it makes its pilgrimage in hope towards the goal of the heavenly homeland.*

*(Vatican II, Decree on Ecumenism, Unitatis Redintegratio, 2)*

# Picture Credits

P.1     Cott Nero DIV f.93v St. Mark's portrait page 45:St Mark, c.698 AD (manuscript) British Library, London, UK.

P.9     Christ the Redeemer, Source of Life, c.1393-94 (tempera on panel), Byzantine, (14th century) / UmjetnickaGallerija, Skopje, Macedonia / Lauros / Giraudon / The Bridgeman Art Library

P.11     ©Photos.com

P.12     ©Photos.com

P.14     Saint John the Baptist, c. 1450 by Michelozzo © Kimbell Art Museum, Fort Worth, Texas /Art Resource, NY/ Scala, Florence.

P.16     Baptism and Temptation of Jesus by Paolo Veronese. ©Photo Scala, Florence - courtesy of the Ministero Beni e Att. Culturali.

P.17     Christ the Redeemer, Rio de Janeiro, Brazil. Photo ©2001-2009 by Corbis Corporation.

P.18     Corbis Picture Library, London.

P.19     iStockphoto Picture Library.

P.20     ©BiblePlaces.com

P.22     ©Bibleplaces.com

P.24     ©Bibleplaces.com

P.27     Healing of a man possessed by a demon by Vittore Carpaccio. ©Photo Scala, Florence - courtesy of the Ministero Beni e Att. Culturali.

P.30     ©Photos.com

P.31     ©Stock.Xchng

P.32     The Parable of the Sower (April or September), by Abel Grimer, (c.1570-p.1619) / © The Bowes Museum, Barnard Castle, County Durham, UK / The Bridgeman Art Library.

P.34     The Parable of the Sower by James Tissot. © SuperStock, Inc. / SuperStock.

P.37     October Scene in Stone Calendar at Baptistery of Parma. © David Lees/CORBIS.

P.38     iStockphoto Picture Library.

P.41     ©BiblePlaces.com

P.42     ©Photos.com

P.43     Farming - ©Photos.com.
         Persistence - iStockphoto Picture Library.

P.44     Fol.59v Christ Feeds the Five Thousand (vellum), Italian School, (15th century) / Biblioteca Reale, Turin, Italy / Alinari / The Bridgeman Art Library.

P.44     MS CCC 410 f.67 Christ walking on the waves, from an illuminated copy of 'Meditations on the Life of Christ' by St. Bonaventure (1221-74) Italian,© Corpus Christi College, Oxford, UK / The Bridgeman Art Library.

# Notes

# Notes

# Notes

# Notes